THE CULT
THAT CALLS ITSELF

THE CHURCH OF CHRIST

What everyone needs to know
about what they teach.

by

Ronald Craig

Pastor of

Living Way Fellowship

Copyright © 2021 by Ronald Craig

All rights reserved. No part of this publication may be reproduced, distributed, or transmitted in any form or by any means, including photocopying, recording, or other electronic or mechanical methods, without the prior written permission of the publisher, except in the case brief quotations embodied in critical reviews and other noncommercial uses permitted by copyright law.

ISBN: 978-1-63945-195-1 (Paperback)
        978-1-63945-196-8 (Hardback)
        978-1-63945-203-3 (Ebook)

The views expressed in this book are solely those of the author and do not necessarily reflect the views of the publisher, and the publisher hereby disclaims any responsibility for them.

Writers' Branding
1800-608-6550
www.writersbranding.com
orders@writersbranding.com

Unless otherwise noted, *ALL* Scripture references are taken from the King James Bible Version; with some rewording for clarity. Within Scripture quotations, words in *italics* and/or *ALL CAPITALS* are this author's emphases. And some of the author's own words are in either *italics* or *ALL CAPITALS* for emphasis regarding certain Bible Truths.

KJV—King James Version

NRSV—New Revised Standard Version.

Contents

	Introduction	3
I	Church of Christ water-baptism heresy—One	5
II	Church of Christ water-baptism heresy—Two	9
III	Church of Christ water-baptism heresy—Three	11
IV	More honest passages dishonestly distorted	13
V	Non-water-baptism salvation passages	17
VI	Other water-baptism passages	21
VII	Religious downplay of the miraculous	25
VIII	Permanent Bible stance on the miraculous	29
IX	At the foot of the cross and the Last Adam	37
X	Taking on the first Adam and his problems	43
XI	Why Church of Christ doctrine comes up short—A	49
XII	Why Church of Christ doctrine comes up short—B	55
XIII	Other serious Church of Christ errors—A	65
XIV	Other serious Church of Christ errors—B	69
XV	Other serious Church of Christ errors—C	77
XVI	Some silly Church of Christ doctrines	81
XVII	Miscellaneous misunderstandings	85
	Conclusion—Summary of the principle parts	89

Acknowledgments

I acknowledge first of all Jesus Christ, my Lord and Savior, Who has given me all the revelation contained in this book. I also want to thank my wife, Joan, and the other members of **Living Way Fellowship** for their sustained patience and support of me in all my authoring endeavors. May this book and all of my other publications honor each of them.

Introduction

Why do I call the Church of Christ a "cult"? *The general definition of the term CULT is: A group of people who follow a human leader, or has a questionable doctrinal stance.* In the case of the Church of Christ, both descriptions fit perfectly.

Although that denomination (*and they claim they are not a denomination*) was actually begun back in the early 1800s in the Barton/Stone revival in Kentucky and Tennessee, the members of that church outright deny that historical truth, and claim instead they are *the same church which began on the day of Pentecost*. But, in reality, there is no resemblance whatsoever between the two. The Church of Christ is about as different from the early church as a church can get!

What is known today as the *Church of Christ* was started by *Alexander Campbell* in the early 1800s, although most in that church try to distance themselves from *the real history of their beginning, and from their human founder, Alexander Campbell*. Early on, and for some time, the members of that church were called Campbellites by outsiders. *And, the term became grossly offensive to those who wanted to believe that they represented the true Christianity of the first century.* So they chose to lie about their actual historical roots.

And, what about those questionable doctrines? They will be scripturally proven in this book to be *outright falsehoods*. So let us now begin to investigate the Church of Christ false doctrines; then prove beyond question that they are false by checking out *numerous eye-opening Scripture passages* that teach the *BIBLE TRUTH* about *water-baptism, miracles,* and several other Church of Christ *misrepresentations*.

Chapter One

Church of Christ water-baptism heresy—One

The *worst fallacy* of those Church of Christ preachers is their outright lies regarding the biblical truth of John 3:3-5. *They heretically claim that Jesus Christ taught there that the sinner's spirit becomes regenerated BY water-baptism—That the spirit is born again, placed in the Body of Christ, and into the kingdom of God, BY BOTH water-baptism and Holy Spirit activity.* Satan himself is behind those ungodly conclusions from those Bible verses—which clearly teach *OTHERWISE!*

First of all, Jesus never mentioned water-baptism in His conversation with Nicodemus. When Jesus told him that he must be born *again,* Nicodemus took it that Jesus meant he had to be *born as a baby the second time*—thus two natural births. The Lord assured Nicodemus that when He said the man had to be born *AGAIN, He was talking about a different kind of birth—a spiritual re-birth*—accomplished by the Holy Spirit working within the *SPIRIT* of Nicodemus. In verse six, Jesus clearly explained it—*That which is born of the flesh is flesh, and that which is born of the Holy Spirit is spirit*—two different kinds of birth—*natural birth by water, and spiritual re-birth of our spirit by the Holy Spirit.* That is Bible Truth!

When the Lord said that we must be *born of BOTH water and Spirit,* He obviously meant that we were *already born of water at our natural birth when we came into this old world. The Kingdom of God is entered by the spiritual re-birth of the sinner's lost spirit by the inner operation of the Holy Spirit.*

Now think: The very term *AGAIN* necessitates two births; not two elements of the same birth. They do *NOT* take place at the same time. *We cannot get born AGAIN unless we have been born ALREADY. Birth by water is birth of the flesh from a mother's womb.* So obviously, one must have been *born of the flesh—that is by water—to enter this world—which is the first birth.* Then one's spirit has to be *RE-BORN* by the Spirit of God to get into the Kingdom of God! That is John 3:3-6.

But, in a 400+ page book *written by a prominent Church of Christ theologian on CURRENT Church of Christ teachings,* the author claims that in John 3:3-5, Jesus was referring to two different elements involved in the new birth—water and Spirit. *That is an outright theological LIE—proven by the very wording of that passage itself!* Remember, right after stating in verse five that one has to be born of water *AND* the spirit, *the Lord explained in verse six that "what is born of the flesh is flesh, and what is born of the Spirit is spirit."* Thus, Christ was differentiating between the two births, not teaching two elements of one birth. Birth into the Kingdom of God occurs in our spirits by the Holy Spirit regenerating our spirits; not by our *BODIES* being immersed under water. *That Church of Christ doctrine is one big lie—taught to multitudes of church members in that denomination—which they contend is NOT a denomination.* More exposure of that *LIE* in coming pages.

Although the author of that book brought out some good points, *which the Bible actually teaches (and I learned some good things on certain Bible topics by reading it*—which took me quite a while to finish), all the good things he mentioned were stacked atop that *false-doctrine* foundation. I would be reading along and thrill over some of his biblical points, and then the author would just blast alway all of that good stuff *by saying some of the most stupid and ungodly things about certain Scriptures.* And then I would get angry at that man's dishonest dealings with those passages. It is mind-boggling that preachers and theologians can be so right about some scriptural teachings, *and then be so unbiblical about others.* One thing that fools many believers is that *those preachers have the same enthusiasm for both their lies and Bible Truth.*

Another biblical reality is that the term "born again" may also be translated *"born from above."* Some Bibles point that out in the footnotes. The same Greek word in John 19:11 is rendered "from above"—*when Jesus told Pilate that he could have no authority over Him had it not been given to him from above.* In our new birth, our spirit is *born from above* by the Holy Spirit, Who is from above. *Our water-birth occurs when we come into this natural world.* John 3:3-6 talks about two different kinds of birth; *NOT* two elements of the new birth!

Jesus was *contrasting* the two births: That which is born of the flesh is flesh; that which is born of the Spirit is spirit. Natural birth is by water. When the water bag the baby is in breaks, that baby will soon be born. Birth by the Holy Spirit takes place in a person's spirit—one's inner man. *Thus, the new birth is wholly a matter of the human spirit. There is no connection between submersing one's body in water and the Holy Spirit recreating the inner man. Water-baptism portrays that redemption which has already taken place through faith in a person's spirit. There is no such thing as regeneration by water! Thus, the Church of Christ doctrine that immersion of the physical body in water produces salvation is a DEMONIC DOCTRINE—which Paul warned us about in* 1 Timothy 4:1.

Many Scripture passages discuss water-baptism, and we will deal with many of them as we go along. But, I needed to establish up front that one of the *primary passages used by the Church of Christ preachers to teach that water-baptism is essential to salvation actually teaches the opposite! They say that no one is saved until they get water-baptized. That is an outright Church of Christ lie. Many Scripture passages prove conclusively that the church of Christ Water-baptism doctrine DECEIVES PEOPLE into trusting something for their salvation that cannot produce salvation—making it a demonic doctrine.*

This chapter has dealt with the *WHAT* of water-baptism: *WHAT* water-baptism *SUPPOSEDLY* accomplishes in and for the believer. Supposedly, *WATER-BAPTISM gets a believer's SINS FORGIVEN*, gets him or her *BORN AGAIN*, and *FILLED WITH THE HOLY SPIRIT*. That is Church of Christ doctrine.

The following chapter exposes the Church of Christ *LIES* about *WHEN all of those blessings become ours*. God's clear Word settles that issue as well!

Chapter Two

Church of Christ water-baptism heresy—Two

Another Scripture passage that blows away the teaching that *one's salvation cannot occur until one is water-baptized* is Acts 10:44-48: "While Peter was speaking those words [of the Gospel], *the Holy Ghost fell upon all them who heard the word* [those Gentiles who had gathered in Cornelius' house]. And those of the circumcision [those Jewish believers] were astonished, as many as came with Peter, because, upon the Gentiles also was poured out the gift of the Holy Ghost. For, they *HEARD* them all speak with tongues and magnify God. Then, Peter asked [the Jewish believers]: 'Can anyone forbid water, that these should not be baptized, *who have received the Holy Ghost AS WELL AS WE* [Jewish believers have]?' So he commanded them to be baptized [in water] *in the name of the Lord* [Jesus]." Holy Ghost *FIRST—THEN* water-baptism!

One interesting fact in this event is that, in that sermon, *Peter touched on divine healing before saying anything about forgiveness of sins*: Acts 10:38: "How God anointed Jesus of Nazareth with the Holy Ghost, and power—Who went about doing good, and healing all who were oppressed of the devil; for God was with Him [Jesus]." (Not just a side-issue!)

Peter finally mentioned sins in Acts 10:43: "To Him give all the prophets witness, that through His name, whosoever *BELIEVES* on Him will receive remission of sins." *That was WHEN the Holy Spirit fell on those Gentiles, and they started speaking in tongues and glorifying God. Afterward they were water-baptized.* That is most significant, because,...

Church of Christ preachers insist that *no one is actually saved UNTIL they get water-baptized. But, the Holy Spirit fell on those Gentile believers BEFORE they got water-baptized* —as Acts 10:44-46 clearly tells us. *Was that AN EXCEPTION to the Bible rule*, or is there more here than meets the eye?

Church of Christ preachers *DO CLAIM* that event was an exception to the rule—because it was necessary to point out to the Jewish believers who had come along with Peter that *God had accepted Gentiles into the church.* In this case, God allowed those Gentiles to receive the Holy Spirit before they were water-baptized. But, *if it is true that salvation does not kick in until the believer is water-baptized, then those Gentile believers received the Holy Spirit before they got saved.* That is the obvious conclusion of that Church of Christ doctrine.

Let us consider another Scripture passage the author of that book I read *conveniently failed to point out.* John 14:17 says *the world cannot receive the Holy Spirit.* Now, the *world* in this verse has to refer to the *unsaved.* Christ said plainly that *sinners cannot receive the Holy Spirit.* But, those people in Cornelius' house that day *DID* receive the Holy Spirit. So, those people got saved *BEFORE* they got water-baptized!

And whether the Gentiles received the Holy Spirit at their water-baptism or before it, either would have been proof that they were welcomed into the church. So that exception theory propagated by Church of Christ preachers is proven FALSE. Religiousites do that same thing every time their theological nonsense gets *exposed by the Scriptures.* They have to come up with some new lies in an attempt to cover all their other lies. *The forgiveness of sins, the new birth, and receiving the Holy Spirit DO NOT HAVE TO WAIT on one's water-baptism!*

Another Scripture passage that blasts away the Church of Christ doctrine that it is *AT* water-baptism that believers receive the entire salvation package (forgiveness of sins, the new birth, and the Holy Spirit) is Acts 8:14-17. *The when in this case had to do with the reception of the Holy spirit.* "Now when the twelve apostles, at Jerusalem, heard Samaria had received the word of God [having *received* the Gospel means that they were saved], they sent to Samaria Peter and John: Who, when they had come down, prayed for those believers, that they might receive the Holy Ghost: (For, as yet, He had fallen on none of them: Only *they were baptized in the name of the Lord Jesus.*) *Then* they laid their hands on them, and they received the Holy Ghost." Here is an occasion in which believers received the Holy Spirit *AFTER* water-baptism.

Chapter Three

Church of Christ water-baptism heresy—Three

This chapter points out Scripture passages that deal not only with *when* believers usually receive the Holy Spirit, but *HOW* the Holy Spirit is normally imparted to believers.

Church of Christ preachers CONTEND that the Holy Spirit enters the believer AT THE TIME he or she is water-baptized. Thus, according to Church of Christ doctrine, *that is HOW believers get Holy-Spirit-baptized. It is ALWAYS connected to their water-baptism. Holy-Spirit-baptism only occurs when a believer is immersed in water.* So, being baptized in water is HOW the believer gets Holy-Spirit-baptized. However, there are Scripture passages that contradict that flimsy doctrine. So once again, they fall back on that *EXCEPTION* argument. Of course, none of those exceptions apply to us today—they insist. Those few *biblical exceptions* were not to be repeated. How convenient to claim something which cannot be proven one way or the other! We just have to take their word for it. *Yet, we will be judged NOT BY PREACHERS' WORDS, but by God's words.* One of those *supposed* biblical exceptions,...

Down in Samaria, Peter and John laid they their hands upon those who *had believed, AND had been water-baptized* (but had not yet received the Holy Spirit); and they received the Holy Spirit *through the laying on of the apostle's HANDS; and that long after they had been water-baptized—NOT at or by their water-baptism.* This is one of several cases in which the Holy Spirit was imparted by the *LAYING ON OF HANDS;* not by the believer's water-baptism! Another passage:

When Simon the sorcerer saw that *through the laying on of the apostles' hands* the Holy Ghost had been given to the new Christians in Samaria, he offered the apostles *MONEY;* saying: "Give me also that power, so that on whomever *I lay my hands,* he may receive the Holy Ghost (Acts 8:17-19)."

Now, consider Acts 19:2-7, *where the Apostle Paul found some disciples in Ephesus who did not fit the New Testament pattern for SPIRIT-FILLED believers.* Paul asked them: "*Have you received the Holy Ghost SINCE you believed?*" Then they answered: "We have not so much as heard whether there be any Holy Ghost." So Paul then asked them: "*Unto what then were you baptized?*" Then they said: "Unto John's baptism." Then, Paul said: "John [the Baptizer] truly baptized with the baptism of repentance [in water], saying to the crowds that they should believe on Him Who would come after him; that is, on Christ Jesus." When they heard that truth, *they were baptized* [in water] *in the name of the Lord Jesus. And when Paul had LAID HIS HANDS on them,* the Holy Ghost came on them; and they spoke with tongues and prophesied. And all the men were about twelve. Those twelve had been baptized in water, *but the Holy Spirit did not fall upon them until Paul LAID HIS HANDS on them.* These cases bash that Church of Christ doctrine that claims *water-baptism is both the WHEN and the HOW of the believer's Holy-Spirit-reception.*

Another Scripture, *which discredits that Church of Christ misguided doctrine,* is Acts 9:17-18: "Ananias went his way, and entered into the house [where Saul of Tarsus was]; and *PUTTING HIS HANDS ON HIM,* said: 'Brother Saul, the Lord Jesus, Who appeared to you on the road, as you came here, has sent me, that you might receive your sight, and be filled with the Holy Ghost.' And immediately there fell from Saul's eyes as it had been scales: And he received sight forthwith, and [then] arose, and was baptized [in water]."

Notice that Ananias *LAID HIS HANDS on Saul* and called him brother (*not just a brother Jew, but a brother Christian*); and *THEN* Saul's eyes were immediately and totally healed. And since Ananias had said he came so that Saul would be healed *AND be filled with the Holy Spirit*, we have to assume that his Holy-Spirit-infilling occurred when Ananias laid his hands on Saul—just like his healing did. And then, Saul got up and was water-baptized! Holy Spirit *FIRST—THEN* water! Once again, the Holy Spirit *was imparted by the laying on of hands.* Therefore, the Church of Christ doctrine concerning the *WHEN* and *HOW* of Holy-Spirit-baptism is *ERRONEOUS! How many errors will they be allowed to get away with?*

Chapter Four

More honest passages dishonestly distorted

The big one is Titus 3:5: "Not by works of righteousness, which we have done, *but according to God's mercy He saved us, by the washing of regeneration* and *renewing of the Holy Ghost.*" That Church of Christ author appealed to the *NRSV* to make his doctrinal case: "God saved us *through the water of re-birth, and the renewal of the Holy Spirit." Do you detect the obvious difference between that Bible version and that of the KJV above?* I checked out a more literal Bible version as well, and found that *it coincides with the KJV.* Let us look at the major flaw in both that *NRSV* rendering and the Church of Christ teaching. Both imply that regeneration is *obtained by water*—re-birth by *WATER.* The more literal (and honest) rendering is "*by the WASHING of REGENERATION.*" Can you see the difference? In the literal rendering, *it is regeneration that accomplishes the washing, rather than the washing that accomplishes the regeneration.* Regeneration *IS* the washing! *We are washed from sin by being regenerated.* In Titus 3:5, *the Greek word for neither water nor baptism appears.* Thus, *BOTH* the *NRSV* wording in that passage and the Church of Christ doctrine are grossly dishonest. Also, renewing *OF* the Holy Ghost could be rendered renewing *BY* the Holy Ghost. Therefore, washing *OF* regeneration could also be rendered washing *BY* regeneration. In either case, regeneration is not accomplished by water-baptism. It is by the Holy Spirit!

First Corinthians 6:9-10 presents a long list of diabolical sins; and in verse 11, Paul said to the *Corinthian Christians*: "And such [terrible sinners] were some of you: But you were *washed* [How were they washed?]; but you were sanctified; but you were justified in the name of the Lord Jesus Christ, and by the Holy Spirit of our God." *Water does not wash our sins away!* Revelation 1:5 tells us exactly what washes our sins away! "*Unto Him* [Jesus] *Who loved us, and washed us from our sins in His own blood...*" Water cannot touch sins!

Hebrews 10:22 says: "Let us draw near [God] with a true heart in full assurance of faith, having our hearts [meaning our spirits] SPRINKLED *from an evil conscience.*" But how?

In the spirit realm we get sprinkled by the blood of Jesus; not immersed in it. In the natural realm, we get immersed in water, not sprinkled with it—and not to receive salvation, but to testify that we have ALREADY BEEN SAVED through faith. Water cannot touch an evil conscience, for the conscience is on the inside of us, whereas, *water is the natural substance known as H2O, and can only be applied to the human body.* Natural substances do not touch the spirit realm where sin resides. So our spirits do not get born again by water. Jesus said that a person produces evil from the storehouse of evil dwelling within the spirit. See Matthew 12:35, 15:18-19 and Mark 7:20-23. *Spiritual problems require spiritual solutions.*

Church of Christ preachers tend to view EVERY passage that contains the word baptism as a water-baptism passage. Even those Scriptures that refer to Holy-Spirit-baptism they somehow connect to water-baptism. First Corinthians 12:13 tells it like it really is. *"By one SPIRIT [that is the Holy Spirit] we are all BAPTIZED INTO ONE BODY* [the Body of Christ], *whether we are Jews or Gentiles, and, whether we are bond or free; and have all been made to drink into one Spirit* [the Holy Spirit]." Their contention is that, Spirit-baptism occurs *AT* water-baptism, *which places us into Christ.* This passage teaches that we are made part of the Body of Christ *BY THE HOLY SPIRIT, NOT BY OUR WATER-BAPTISM*; and even that not necessarily when we get water-baptized.

First Peter 3:19-21 is one more passage those Church of Christ preachers tamper with: "Christ went and preached to those spirits in prison [Sheol]; which were disobedient when the long-suffering of God waited in Noah's day while the ark was being prepared—wherein few, that is eight, souls, were *SAVED* by water. *The like figure* [the antitype] *even baptism does also now save us (not the putting away of the filth of the flesh, but the answer of a good conscience toward God)."* Noah was inside the ark; not in the flood. So how could Peter have been saying that IMMERSION in water saves us?

Now there are three different types of baptism, with each having three elements. In water-baptism the three elements are: *The baptizer, the one being baptized,* and *the element in which the baptizee is being baptized*: Usually some preacher does the baptizing, a new believer is the one being baptized, and water is the element into which the believer is baptized: *One human being immersing another human being in water.* But think: *If water-baptism saves the one being baptized,* as the Church of Christ claims, *and if the water produces that salvation, then the person doing the baptizing is the savior of the one he, or she, is baptizing. Would that not be the logical conclusion of that Church of Christ water-baptism-doctrine?*

The second type is *the spiritual baptism of a believer into the Body of Christ.* In that unique baptism the Holy Spirit is the *Baptizer*, the *believer* is the one the Holy Spirit baptizes, and the element into which the believer gets baptized is *the Body of Christ.* First Corinthians 12:13 says the Holy Spirit baptizes (immerses) us into one Body—the Body of Christ.

Galatians 3:27-29 adds to that: "*As many of you as have been baptized into Christ have put on Christ*—Where there is neither Jew, Greek, bond, free, male or female: Because you are all one in Christ Jesus. And if you belong to Christ then you are also Abraham's seed, and therefore heirs according to the promise [made to Abraham]." That Greek phrase "put on" actually means "to clothe oneself with." And that means we are *inside Christ!* "*If any man or woman is IN CHRIST*, he or she is a new Creature (2 Corinthians 5:17)." *Inside job!*

The third type of *BAPTISM* is the believer being baptized *WITH* the Holy Spirit. Matthew 3:11: "I, [John the Baptizer], indeed *baptize you with water unto repentance*: But He Who comes after me is mightier than I am: Whose shoes I am not worthy to bear. He [Jesus Christ] will baptize you *WITH* the Holy Ghost, and with fire." Basically the same is repeated in Mark 1:8, Luke 3:16, John 1:33. The Greek word "*EN*" may be rendered *in, with,* or *by*—the context determining which.

In this case, *Jesus is the Baptizer, the believer is the one being baptized,* and *the Holy Spirit is the element into which the believer is being immersed. Three different baptisms,* and *three different entities involved in each different baptism.* Yet

15

the Church of Christ adamantly contends that there is only one baptism—water-baptism. And they base their argument on Ephesians 4:5, which does plainly say that there is "One Lord, one faith, and one baptism." But, Hebrews 6:2 speaks "Of the doctrine of *BAPTISMS* [plural], and the laying on of hands, the resurrection of the dead, and eternal judgment." *ALL* three of those *DIFFERENT* baptismal settings—officials, candidates and elements have a common purpose—*Relating us to God in Christ. One of them places believers in the Body of Christ by the Holy Spirit*; one *fills us with the Holy Spirit*; *and one of them*—water-baptism—*testifies to the world what happened to us on the inside when we got born again.*

Some Scripture passages *relate water-baptism to the Old Testament ceremony of circumcision.* Colossians 2:11-13: "In Whom [Christ] also, you [believers] are *circumcised* with the *circumcision made without hands* [pointing to a process that happens on the inside of believers], *in putting off the body of the sins of the flesh by that* [spiritual] *circumcision of Christ*: Buried with Him in [spiritual] baptism, [not water-baptism], wherein also you are risen with him through the faith of the operation of God, Who raised Him from the dead. And you, being dead in your sins, and in the uncircumcision of your flesh, has He [God] quickened [or made alive] together with Him [Christ], having forgiven you all trespasses." *Inside job!*

Romans 6:3-5: "We who were baptized into Jesus Christ [*by the Holy Spirit, not water-baptism*—1 Corinthians 12:13] were baptized into His death. So we are *BURIED* with Christ by that baptism into death: That, just like Christ was raised from the dead, by the glory of the Father, so also we should walk in newness of life. Because, if we have been *PLANTED* together in the likeness of His *DEATH*, we will also be in the likeness of His resurrection." *We bury only people ALREADY DEAD!* Water-baptism pictures our death to sin with Christ, and *our spirit having been raised from the dead* with Him.

Acts 15:8-9: "And God Who knows the hearts bore them witness by giving them the Holy Ghost, just as He did to us: And *put no difference between us and the* [Gentile believers], *purifying their hearts BY FAITH* [*NOT* by water-baptism]."

Chapter Five

Non-water-baptism salvation passages

Acts 16:29-34: After the earthquake occurred at the jail, which loosed all the shackles from the prisoners, that jailer "called for a light, then sprang in, and came trembling, then fell down before Paul and Silas, then brought them out, and said: 'Sirs, what must I do to be saved?' And they answered: '*BELIEVE upon the Lord Jesus Christ, and you will be saved*, and your house.' And they spoke unto the jailer the Word of the Lord, and unto all who were in his house. Then, he took them that same hour of the night, and washed their stripes; and was baptized, he and all his, straightway. And when he had brought them into his house, he set meat before them, and rejoiced, believing in God with all of his house [family]."

Since the jailer and all his family got water-baptized, *it is OBVIOUS that Paul spoke of water-baptism to those people.* But the biblical point I make here, and will keep on making, is that, *if our salvation is vitally linked to our water-baptism, like the Church of Christ preachers contend, then why did it not get mentioned in EVERY CASE of Gospel preaching?* Paul answered that man's query with, "*Believe on the Lord Jesus Christ and you will be saved*, along with your whole house." Paul said nothing about water-baptism in that first answer.

Romans 10:8-11: "What does [the righteousness of faith] say? [So, the righteousness of faith talks.] The word is near you, even in your *mouth* and in your *heart: That is the word of faith which we preach:* [Which is:] *If you confess with your mouth that Jesus is Lord, and believe in your heart that God has raised Him from the dead, THEN you will be saved.* For, with the *heart* a man believes unto righteousness; and with the *mouth* confession is made unto salvation. Because, the Bible says that: '*Whosoever BELIEVES upon Him will not be ashamed* [or put to shame].'" *If water-baptism is essential to our salvation, then why did Paul not include it with believing and confessing? Church of Christ doctrine is a demonic lie!*

Romans 3:22: "Even the righteousness of God, *which IS BY THE FAITH OF JESUS CHRIST*; to all, and on all, people who *BELIEVE*: For, there is no difference." In this verse, the words righteousness, faith, and believe are mentioned, but not water-baptism. *Church of Christ doctrine is eroding!!!*

Romans 4:5: "But to him who works not, but *believes* on Him [God], Who justifies the ungodly, *his faith is counted for righteousness*." Faith, not water-baptism, is righteousness.

Romans 4:9-11: "Does that blessedness come upon the circumcision only, or upon the uncircumcision also? For we say that *FAITH was reckoned to Abraham for righteousness*. How was it then reckoned? When he was in circumcision or in uncircumcision [after he was circumcised, or before]? Not in circumcision, but in uncircumcision. And he received the sign of circumcision, a seal of the *righteousness of the faith, which he had while he was yet uncircumcised*; that he might be the father of all those who *BELIEVE*, though they are not circumcised; *so that righteousness might be imputed to them too*." *Righteousness is not by circumcision or water-baptism!*

Romans 4:21-24: "Being fully persuaded that what He [God] had promised, He was able also to perform. And so, it was imputed to Abraham for righteousness. Now, it was not written for his sake alone, that it was imputed to him—But for us also to whom it will be imputed if we *BELIEVE* upon Him Who raised Jesus Christ our Lord from the dead."

John 20:31: "These things are written, so that you might *BELIEVE* that Jesus is the Christ, the Son of God; and that *BELIEVING you may have life through His name*." (No water!)

Acts 4:4: "Howbeit many of them who heard the Word [of the Gospel] *believed*; and the number of the men was about five thousand." *No mention of water-baptism in this passage either*, though the event occurred after Acts 2:38. Why not?

Acts 10:43: "Whoever *believes* on Him [Jesus Christ] will receive *remission of sins*." *No mention of water-baptism here in connection with remission of sins*. Again, why not?

Acts 13:38-39: "Through Jesus is preached unto you the *forgiveness of sins*: Through Him *all those who BELIEVE are justified from all things from which you could not be justified by the law of Moses.*" Forgiveness WITHOUT water-baptism!

Romans 1:16: "I am not ashamed of the *Gospel of Christ*: *For it* [the Gospel] *is the power of God unto salvation to every one who BELIEVES—to the Jew first; and also to the Greek.*" To those who *BELIEVE*—Water-baptism not mentioned!

Romans 3:26: "That God might be just, and the *Justifier of him who BELIEVES on Jesus.*" Another passage, in which water-baptism is not even mentioned; let alone emphasized!

Romans 10:4: "For Jesus Christ is the end of the law for righteousness to everyone who *BELIEVES*." *No connection of righteousness with water here—or anywhere else!*

Ephesians 1:13: "*In Whom* [Christ] *you also trusted, after you heard the Word of truth, the Gospel of your salvation*: In Whom also, after you *BELIEVED*, you were *sealed with that Holy Spirit of promise.*" So, *that Holy-Spirit-sealing-operation was connected to BELIEVING*—not to water-baptism.

First Timothy 4:10: "We both labour and suffer reproach because we trust in the Living God; Who is the Savior of all men; *especially of those who BELIEVE.*" Where is the water?

First John 5:1 says: "*Whosoever BELIEVES that Jesus is the Christ is born of God.*" Being *BORN AGAIN* without being water-baptized! Was John ignorant of that *Church of Christ water-baptism-doctrine? Are they smarter than John?*

First Corinthians 1:17: "*Christ sent me* [the Apostle Paul] *not to baptize* [with water], *but to preach the Gospel.*" Now, *if water-baptism really is ESSENTIAL to salvation, Paul did not get many people saved—according to* 1 Corinthians 1:14-17.

Acts 17:11-12: "These [Israelites] were more noble than those in Thessalonica, in that *they received the Word of God with all readiness of mind,* and *they searched the Scriptures daily, whether those things* [Paul taught] *were so.* Therefore, many of them *BELIEVED*; even honorable Greek women and men, not a few." No water-baptism teaching recorded here.

Acts 17:34: "Howbeit certain men clave unto him [Paul], and *BELIEVED*: Which included Dionysius the Areopagite, a woman named Damaris, and a few others with them." Once again, no mention of water-baptism in this passage.

First Corinthians 1:21: "After that in the wisdom of God, *the world by its wisdom knew not God, it pleased God by the foolishness of preaching to save all those who BELIEVE.*" No mention of water-baptism here either. *Water cannot save!*

Galatians 3:22: "The Scripture has concluded *ALL* under sin, so that, the promise *BY FAITH* of Jesus Christ might be given to all who *BELIEVE*." What happened to the water?

Philemon 1:10: "I beseech you for *MY SON* [in the faith], Onesimus, *whom I have BEGOTTEN* [got born again] *in my bonds*." Paul had gotten Onesimus *SAVED* sometime during his two-year imprisonment in Rome. *Paul was under house arrest and could not leave the premises.* So, if water-baptism has to occur before one is born again, how did Paul get that man saved? *Surely that rental house had no baptismal pool.* Onesimus must have been a prisoner too; and living in that same *HIRED HOUSE* with Paul. Notice that *Paul had to PAY RENT to live in his own prison cell* (Acts 28:30)!

Now, that Scripture passage even more well-known than Acts 2:38, John 3:14-16 states: "Just as Moses lifted up the [bronze] serpent in the wilderness, even so must the Son of man be lifted up: So that, whoever *BELIEVES* in Him should not perish, but have eternal life. For, God so loved the world that He gave His *only-begotten Son*, that *whoever BELIEVES in Him should not perish but have everlasting life.*" There are more Scriptures that prove the same truth, but I believe the ones I have presented are sufficient to get the point across.

Chapter Six

Other water-baptism passages

Acts 2:37-39: "When they heard that, they were pricked in their heart and said to Peter and to those other apostles, 'Men and brethren, what must we do?' Then Peter said unto them, 'Repent and be baptized every one of you in the name of Jesus Christ for the remission of your sins, and you will receive the gift of the Holy Ghost. For, the promise is to you, and to your children, and to all who are afar off [in time and location], even as many as the Lord our God will call.'"

If this were the only passage speaking to this issue, then we might agree with the *Church of Christ* doctrine. However, those Scriptures in the previous chapters of this book blast away *their claim that salvation cannot occur UNTIL a person is water-baptized. I have found that no ONE Scripture is ALL the Bible! Study all that the Bible has to say about a subject before making a conclusion on that subject*—especially before going public with your conclusion. Look at 2 Timothy 2:15: "*Study to show yourself approved unto God, a workman who needs not to be ashamed, rightly dividing the word of truth.*" *That tells me that if I do not put forth some study effort, I will end up being ashamed—and will do DISSERVICE to God and His church.* I do not want that on my conscience.

There are two more passages they contend validate their *water-salvation doctrine.* One is Mark 16:15-16: "The Lord said unto them: '*Go into all the world, and preach the Gospel to every creature. He who believes, and is baptized, will be saved*: But, those who believe not will be condemned.'" That passage also *SEEMS TO MAKE THEIR CASE. But, remember all those passages that promise salvation by simply believing the Gospel message—with no mention of water-baptism—the most well-known being* John 3:16. If salvation is locked into the believer *ONLY* when he or she gets water-baptized, *that point ought to be made in every passage promising salvation!*

That third *supposedly convincing passage* the Church of Christ theologians use to push their doctrine is John 3:3-5: "Jesus answered and said to Nicodemus, 'Truly, truly,' I say unto you: 'Except a man be *BORN AGAIN*, he cannot see the Kingdom of God.' Nicodemus answered: 'How can a man be born when he is old? Can he enter the *second time* into his mother's womb, and be born?' Jesus answered him, 'Truly, truly,' I say unto you, 'Except a man be born of *WATER* and the *SPIRIT* he cannot enter into the Kingdom of God.'"

If you go back and re-read chapter one, you will see why that verse cannot be used to push their false water-baptism doctrine. To be *BORN AGAIN* obviously means that one has been born once *ALREADY*. Thus, *Jesus could not have been teaching that being born of water meant that water-baptism births one into the Kingdom of God!* Water-birth occurs when we are born into this world as a human being. Natural birth is by water. *Nicodemus ASSUMED that Jesus meant one had to be born of water TWO TIMES. Christ straightened him out by telling him we must experience a different kind of birth, in order to enter the Kingdom of God—a spiritual re-birth.* Now, we humans are *ALREADY* born of water—*WHICH DID NOT PUT US IN THE KINGDOM OF GOD!* We also have to be born of the Holy *SPIRIT*. Jesus explained that in John 3:6: "*What is born of the flesh is FLESH, and what is born of the Spirit is SPIRIT.*" The Savior emphasized two different kinds of birth; which occur at different times—*not two activities involved in the new birth at the same time.* That destroys the Church of Christ water-baptism doctrine—which is an outright lie!

Acts 2:41: "Those who gladly received Peter's words were *baptized; and there were added to them that day about three thousand souls.*" Added before, at, or after water-baptism?

Acts 8:12-13: "But, when they believed Philip, preaching those things concerning the Kingdom of God, and the name of Jesus Christ, they were *baptized*, both men, and women. Then, Simon [the sorcerer] himself *believed* also: And, when he too was *baptized*, he followed Philip, and was in wonder, beholding the miracles and signs which Philip did." Pointing out more passages speaking of people being water-baptized.

Acts 8:36-39: "As they went on their way they came unto a certain water: And, the eunuch said to Philip, 'See, here is water; what hinders me from being *baptized?*' Then, Philip said to him, 'If you believe with all your heart you may.' And he answered, and said, *'I believe that Jesus Christ is the Son of God.'* Then he commanded the chariot to stand still: And, they went down into the water, both Philip and the eunuch; and Philip *baptized* him. And when they had come up out of the water, the Spirit of the Lord caught away Philip, so that the eunuch saw him no more: And, the eunuch went on his way rejoicing." *Philip must have mentioned water-baptism to that man*, but there is no indication in that passage that the man was not SAVED BEFORE he was immersed in water.

Acts 18:8: "And Crispus, *the chief ruler of the synagogue*, BELIEVED on the Lord with all his house. And, many of the Corinthian citizens hearing BELIEVED, and were *baptized.*"

First Corinthians 10:1-2: "Brethren I would not that you be ignorant of the fact that our fathers were under the *cloud* [in the wilderness 40 YEARS], and that they passed through the [Red] *sea*; and were all *baptized* unto Moses in the *cloud* and in the *sea.*" Through the Red Sea ONCE, but under the cloud 40 YEARS. *For whatever this is worth—In neither case did the Israelites get wet in those two baptisms.*

There is no doubt that water-baptism is important to the Christian. But *Church of Christ doctrine gives water-baptism an importance the Bible does not.* Several passages we have investigated *PROVE* beyond doubt that those water-baptism recipients were *SAVED PRIOR TO IMMERSION* in water. And some of those believers *RECEIVED* their Holy-Spirit-baptism *BEFORE* they got water-baptized—some afterward. *All those Bible realities blast that heretical Church of Christ doctrine!*

An entire denomination is cursed with the false doctrine, which insists that salvation cannot occur in ones life UNTIL the believer is immersed in water. But think: *Water does not MAKE anyone a believer! The water-baptism candidate must be a believer BEFORE getting into the water.* Otherwise, the ceremony is futile. See Acts 8:37 again for that Bible Truth.

One more baptism-passage the Church of Christ distorts with their *distorted theology* is Acts 22:16; which tells about the disciple named Ananias having been sent to the blinded Saul of Tarsus for the purpose of getting his eye-sight back, and getting him filled with the Holy Spirit. After giving Saul Christ's message, he said to the converted Saul: "And now, what are you waiting for? Arise, and be baptized, [in water], and *wash away your sins—CALLING UPON THE NAME OF THE LORD.*" Of course, they insist this proves water washes away our sins. But does it? In reality, *it is not the water that washes away sins, but rather, OUR CALLING ON THE NAME OF THE LORD!* How can I say that? Because Peter said that! Speaking of the end times, Peter wrote in Acts 2:21: "And, it will come to pass [from Peter's day, right up to the end] that whoever *CALLS ON THE NAME OF THE LORD* will be saved." Peter was quoting from Joel 2:32: "It will come to pass that, whoever *CALLS ON THE NAME OF THE LORD* will be saved." No mention of water-baptism in either passage.

Church of Christ preachers also distort that Bible Truth! *To make that passage fit their doctrinal view, they insist that submitting to water-baptism is the SAME as calling upon the name of the Lord. What a stretch of the religious imagination! How DESPERATE Church of Christ preachers are to maintain their distorted theology. CALLING* upon the name of the Lord requires the use of one's *VOICE*; and that demands that one *BREATH*. It is tuff to breath under water! There seems to be no limit to how far from the Scriptures the Church of Christ preachers will go to hold onto their perverted theology.

Revelation 1:5 says in no uncertain terms that it is *THE BLOOD OF JESUS CHRIST* that washes away sins. And that occurs in our lives when we *CALL UPON THE NAME OF THE LORD IN FAITH! Water is powerless to touch the inner man, where sin resides.* Only spiritual power can resolve spiritual problems. Tamper not with God's Inspired Word!

Chapter Seven

Religious downplay of the miraculous

I have a good biblical reason for dealing with the subject of *miracles* in this chapter; which comes right after those on water-baptism. *Of the three primary passages the Church of Christ uses to promote their water-baptism HERESY*, the one most distorted is John 3:3-5. In fact, they outright lie about what the Lord said in that passage. They say He taught that *our SPIRIT gets born spiritually by our BODY being immersed in water—a chemical substance—while the Holy Spirit works inside our spirit. Water-baptism on the OUTSIDE—Holy Spirit action on the INSIDE—both working together to achieve OUR re-birth—THEY CLAIM. Yet Jesus contrasted natural birth by water with spiritual re-birth by the Holy Spirit—two different kinds of birth, not two components of the new birth.*

Of course, their favorite Scripture passage is Acts 2:38. They obviously think that with that passage and John 3:3-5 they have their argument on solid biblical ground. But, they also appeal to Mark 16:15-16 as a *biblical back-up passage*. However, Mark chapter sixteen exposes yet another flaw in *Church of Christ theology*. In the 400+ page book that I read on *Church of Christ doctrine*, in the back of the book there is *an index of Scripture passages that appear in the book.* Now, Mark 16:15-16 shows up in that index. But verses 17-18 do not. Those verses promise miracles for and by the church.

Some people may claim that the reason for not including those verses, either in the index or in the book itself, is that *the book is not about miracles, but Church of Christ doctrine*. However, in more than one section of that book, the author does talk about miracles—*DENYING* that they are for today! So, Church of Christ doctrine strikes once again by denying God's *MIRACLE* promises. *Why do the Church of Christ and other church groups CHOOSE TO ACCEPT certain portions of the Bible as valid, while REJECTING certain other portions?*

Mark 16:17-18: "And these signs will follow [accompany] those *WHO BELIEVE*; In My [Jesus'] name they will cast out demons; they will speak with new tongues; they will take up serpents; and if they drink any deadly thing, it will not hurt them; they will lay hands on the sick and they will recover."

Many *preachers and denominations* reject Mark 16:9-20, claiming those verses are not part of the inspired Scripture, because they are not in a couple of Greek manuscripts. *But the Church of Christ accepts at least verses 15-16 as VALID. Why do they believe two verses but conveniently deny all the rest?* If they believe that all of Mark 16:9-20 is genuine, why do they shun the miracle portion of that passage? Are those verses not just as *INSPIRED* as all the rest? Could it be that they are just acting out of *religious bias* because they do not want to believe that miracles are for our day; as well as they were for the first century? Do they think they have the right to *choose* what they want to believe and turn their backs on the rest? *Better find out what God's Word says about that!*

One Bible clue: Luke 6:40: "The disciple is not above his Master: But, everyone who is perfect [mature] will be as his Master." Jesus was referring to Himself as the Master. What did He promise all of His followers? *The fully trained disciple* (believer) *will be able to do whatever his Master Jesus Christ did in His earthly ministry.* Christ's church-age promise!

More proof: John 14:12: "Truly, truly, I tell you, He who believes upon Me, the *SAME* works that I do will he do; and even *GREATER* works will he do, because, I go to My Father [and send back the Holy Spirit, to enable believers to do the works I do; and greater]." *Jesus did not limit that promise to either the original twelve apostles, or to believers living in the first century.* That promise is to *ALL* who believe to this day!

Acts 1:8: "*You will receive power after the Holy Spirit has come upon you: And you will be My witnesses* in Jerusalem, and in all of Judaea, and in Samaria, and *to the ends of the earth.*" And again, *that promise was not limited to the twelve apostles, or to believers living in those early days. NOT ONE* of those twelve apostles reached the *ENDS* of this earth. So, *that promise will be good until this earth's ends are reached!*

Acts 8:6-8: "And the people with one accord gave heed to the things Philip spoke, hearing and seeing all the miracles which he did. For, unclean spirits crying out with loud voice came out of many who were possessed by them: And, many people who had the palsy, and who were lame, were healed. And [as a result,] there was *GREAT JOY* in that city."

Acts 9:33-35: "There, Peter found a certain man named Aeneas, who had been bedfast for eight years, and was sick of the palsy. And Peter said unto him: 'Aeneas, Jesus Christ makes you whole: Arise, and make your bed.' Then, Aeneas arose immediately. And, all of those who dwelt at Lydda and Saron saw him [now healed], and *TURNED TO THE LORD.*"

Acts 9:40-42: "Peter put them all out and kneeled down, and prayed: Then, turning to her body, Peter said: 'Tabitha, arise.' Then she opened her eyes: And, when she saw Peter, she sat up. Then Peter gave her his hand and lifted her up; then he called the saints and widows and *presented Tabitha alive.* And that was known throughout all Joppa; and many *BELIEVED IN THE LORD* [because of that healing-miracle]."

I presented these three passages for a couple of reasons. One is that I recently saw on *TV* a denominational preacher telling about Peter's *MIRACLES—then religiously stated that Peter had such gifts, BUT today, we believers do not.* And *he gave no scriptural backing for that COWARDLY COMMENT.* I wanted to scream at that *DECEIVED PREACHER*: "Show me one Scripture that agrees with your *religious cowardice!*"

My second reason for appealing to these three Scripture passages is to expose one more *COWARDLY CLAIM made by most modern preachers—which is that believers exemplifying fortitude in sickness and pain often inspires the lost to accept Christ as their own Savior. In other words, it is sickness that glorifies God and inspires people, according to the majority of today's denominational preachers; including those Church of Christ preachers and theologians. But, those three passages in the book of Acts reveal the very opposite to be true. It was the sick getting MIRACULOUSLY HEALED that glorified God, and persuaded onlookers to accept Jesus Christ as Savior.*

Many more examples of miracles are found in the Gospels and Acts; and we will not shun them in this book. Of course, the miracles Christ performed are prime *EXAMPLES.* Notice that *I called those miracles examples. Examples provide THE PATTERN for what is supposed to FOLLOW after the pattern has been established.* And, that is a biblical principle, found throughout the New Testament. *Jesus did not come to earth and enter His Gospel ministry to put on a three-year miracle show to impress people. No, Christ came to both reveal God's will about all things, including His MIND for miracles, and to establish the pattern for believers to follow after His passion and resurrection.* And that pattern included the inclusion of miracles in Gospel ministry until our Lord's return to earth. You will discover in the New Testament that *GOD HAS* both *PROMISED miracles for believers, and COMMANDED that we believers believe Him for miracles. Not only that; Jesus Christ fussed on whole cities where He had performed miracles, but the citizens of those cities had not repented afterward.*

Matthew 11:20-24: "*Jesus began to rebuke those cities in which MOST OF HIS MIGHTY WORKS [MIRACLE-HEALINGS] had been performed, BECAUSE THEY DID NOT REPENT AND BELIEVE THE GOSPEL THEMSELVES after witnessing all of His miracles. 'WOE unto you, Chorazin! And WOE unto you, Bethsaida! For, if the mighty works which were done in you had been done in Tyre and Sidon, they would have repented long ago, in sackcloth and ashes. But, I say to you: 'IT WILL BE MORE TOLERABLE FOR TYRE AND SIDON ON THE DAY OF JUDGMENT THAN IT WILL BE FOR YOU.'* And, you also, Capernaum, who are exalted to heaven; you will be brought down to Hades: For, if the mighty works which were done in you had been done in Sodom it would have remained to this day. But I say to you that *IT WILL BE MORE TOLERABLE* for Sodom in the day of judgment than it will be for you." In the judgment, what will God say to the people living today, who teach that miracles went away? Many believers are sick and dying unnecessarily today, because *cowardly preachers are preaching cowardly doctrines. I have published a book which differentiates between GENUINE Christian suffering and that which neither glorifies God nor is of any benefit to Christians.* Learn more about it at www.livingwayfellowshiponline.org.

Chapter Eight

Permanent Bible stance on the miraculous

First Corinthians 1:7-8: "So that you come behind in *NO* [Holy Spirit] *GIFT, while waiting for the COMING of our Lord Jesus Christ: Who will confirm you unto the end* [of the age]." Miracles are to continue until Christ's *SECOND COMING!*

First Corinthians 2:4-5: "My speech and preaching were not with enticing words of human wisdom, but instead were in demonstration of the Spirit and power: So that your faith should not stand in the wisdom of men, but in the power of God." *Supernatural power, not ecclesiastical intellectualism!*

First Corinthians 4:20: "For, *the Kingdom of God is not in word only, but also in POWER." The Kingdom of God did not evaporate! Believers are still in the Kingdom of God on earth.* Thus, *the Kingdom-of-God-Power is to be manifested today!*

First Corinthians 12:18: "Now, God has *SET* every one of the members in the body [meaning both the physical body, and the Body of Christ—the church] as it has pleased Him." Now, we cannot imagine God having made some of our body parts to be *merely temporary*. And, since Paul said the same thing about the *Body-of-Christ-parts*, how can anyone claim that some of the *Body-of-Christ-parts* were only temporary?

First Corinthians 12:28 states plainly that "God has *SET* some *IN THE CHURCH*, first apostles, secondarily prophets, thirdly teachers; after that miracles, gifts of healings, helps, governments, diversities of tongues." *ALL of them were SET!*

The Greek word for *SET* means to *PLACE, APPOINT*, and *ORDAIN—NEITHER WORD IMPLYING TEMPORARINESS.* The Apostle Paul used that same word to indicate *God's attitude and actions regarding ALL the Holy Spirit gifts.* None of them have been scheduled to *pass away* during this age.

And, we are told again in Ephesians 4:11-16: "God gave some, apostles; and some, prophets; and some, evangelists; and some, pastors, and teachers; all *for the perfecting of the saints, for the work of ministry, for the EDIFYING of the Body of Christ: UNTIL we ALL come into the UNITY of the faith and the knowledge of the Son of God, TO A PERFECT MAN, to the measure of the STATURE of the FULLNESS of Christ*: That we henceforth be no more children [immature], being tossed to and fro, and carried about by every wind of doctrine, by the sleight of men, and the cunning craftiness, whereby they lie in wait to deceive: But, speaking the truth in love, may grow up into Him, in all things, Who is the Head [of the church], even Jesus Christ: From Whom, the whole body, fitly joined together, and compacted by that which every joint supplies, according to the effectual working in the measure of every part, makes increase of the body of Christ, unto the edifying of itself in love." Paul certainly wrote a mouth-full there!

All of the Holy Spirit gifts were given *UNTIL! Until what? Until we all come into the UNITY of the faith.* To this day that has not happened: *Until we all come unto the measure of the stature of the FULLNESS of Christ*: Will anyone dare say that the church has reached that spiritual height? *Are all of the parts of the Body of Christ working together to EDIFY itself in LOVE?* If we are, then why is today's church splintered into thousands of denominations? *It is obvious that we will need ALL the Holy Spirit GIFTS and MINISTRIES until Jesus Christ returns to earth.* Just from the practical standpoint,...

Today we have *supernatural enemies* just like the church had in its early days—*the devil*, other *fallen angels, demons*, and *demon-possessed humans—whom the devil CONTROLS*. Remember that he is called the "god of this age." Christ said *the devil is the SPIRITUAL father of sinners* (John 8:44). The devil's kids think and act just like he does. So, *to defeat our supernatural enemies, we need supernatural weaponry*.

However, the *general consensus* in the modern church is that all those supernatural gifts and ministries passed away long ago. So we must now depend on other means *TO COPE WITH* our problems. It is *COWARDLY PREACHERS* who lead today's church into that demonic unbelief. They appeal to 1 Corinthians 13:8-12 to supposedly establish their cowardly theological claims—*although that Scripture passage actually teaches the very opposite of their theological contentions.*

So, let us look closely at 1 Corinthians 13:8-12: "Charity [agape—*Greek word for the God-kind of love*] never fails: But whether there be *prophecies*, they will fail; whether there be *tongues*, they will cease; whether there be *knowledge* [gift of the word of knowledge], it will vanish away. For, we know in part, and we prophesy in part. However, when that which is PERFECT has come, then that which is in PART will be done away with. When I [Paul] was a child, I spoke like a child, I understood like a child, I thought like a child: But, when I became a man, I put away childish things. For, *NOW* we see through a [dim] mirror [imperfectly]; but *THEN* [we will see] *face to face: NOW* I know in part; but *THEN I will know even as ALSO I am known.*" Notice that Paul was looking forward to the coming of that which is *PERFECT*. What was it?

Here is the claim of that *Church of Christ author*, as well as most denominational preachers today. I have heard them tell the same old lie over and over. Standard theology claims that when Paul wrote *"when that which is perfect has come,"* he was referring to the completion of all the New Testament books. *When that happens the church will no longer need the gifts of the Holy Spirit, or miracles.* That has to be one of the stupidest statements ever made! *Besides being a slap in the face of every human being who has the same needs today as any human being has ever had, it is also a slap in the face of both God and Jesus Christ, both of Whom were INVOLVED in providing miracles at an extreme price for both of them.* I will not apologize for publicly pointing out that such theological reasoning is *STUPID. And it is actually BLASPHEMOUS! That theological stance actually makes God out to be a LIAR.* But, in reality, those theologians and preachers are the liars! Let the Scriptures themselves demonstrate why that is true.

James 1:23-25: "If anyone is a hearer of *THE WORD OF GOD*, but not a doer [of it], then he is like a man looking at his natural face in a glass [*MIRROR*—the same Greek word used for *MIRROR* in 1 Corinthians 13:12]: Because he looks at himself, then goes away, and straightway he forgets what manner of man he [saw in the mirror]. But, whosoever looks into the *PERFECT LAW* of liberty, and continues therein, *he being not a forgetful hearer but a doer of the word, he will be blessed.*" James called those already-existing Bible books a MIRROR and the PERFECT law of liberty—SAME WORDS in 1 Corinthians 13:8-12. *JAMES being written LONG BEFORE the last New Testament book was [A.D. 98-100], and James being one of the EARLIEST of those New Testament writings, and James calling the already-existing Bible books perfect, Paul must have had something TOTALLY different in mind by "that which is perfect."—The Second Coming of Jesus Christ!*

"*NOW* we *SEE* through a mirror [darkly]; but *THEN*, [we will see] *FACE TO FACE* [when that which is perfect has come]." Before jumping to conclusions, think about this:

When the *last* period was put on the *last* word of the *last* sentence of the *last* New Testament book, *did everyone start seeing face to face? That prophecy fits the Second Coming of Christ, not the completion of the New Testament!*

"*NOW I* [Paul] *know PARTIALLY, but THEN I will know as also I am known.*" Did believers start getting super-intelligent after the LAST pen stroke was made in the LAST book of the New Testament? And think about this as well: Paul said that when that which is perfect has come, *THEN* he would know even as he was known. Well, Paul was beheaded a long time before John wrote the Revelation, and the three little Johns; the *LAST* New Testament books. Paul never experienced on earth "knowing as he was known." *Was that because he did not live until the completion of the New Testament books? Or was he prophesying the Second Coming of Christ—NOT the completion of the New Testament? Got understanding yet?*

The completion of the New Testament enabled nobody to know just as they were known; or to see anything with total clarity. If nothing else proves that, *then surely the thousand years of biblical ignorance called the DARK AGES does. Only when Jesus Christ comes again will we begin to SEE FACE TO FACE and to KNOW AS WE ARE KNOWN.*

This very book is proving that Church of Christ preachers are NOT yet seeing anything face to face, or knowing as they are known by God. Instead, they are *BLIND LEADERS* of the *BLIND*—as Jesus said in Matthew 15:14.

More passages proving that God wants *MIRACLES* right up to the Second Coming of Christ—itself a miracle: Those like Matthew 28:18-20: "Jesus said to them, 'All authority is given unto Me in heaven and in earth. You go therefore, and make disciples of all nations, baptizing them in the name of the Father, the Son, and the Holy Ghost: Teaching them to *OBSERVE EVERYTHING THAT I HAVE COMMANDED YOU*: And, behold, *I AM WITH YOU* always [literally, all the days], *even to the END of the age.*" Christ had commanded them in Matthew 10:8 to *heal the sick, cleanse lepers, raise the dead* and *cast out demons.* Thus all that is *SUPPOSED* to happen, generation after generation, until He returns: Because, *each generation is to make disciples by preaching the Gospel, and then teach the new disciples to continue the SAME ministry.*

Mark 16:20: "They went forth and preached everywhere; *the Lord working WITH them, and confirming the Gospel with accompanying signs* [miracles]." Why would God not want to confirm His Word with miracles in our day? Remember that Jesus said: *"I AM WITH YOU ALL THE DAYS TO THE END!"*

Matthew 18:18-20: "Truly, I say unto you, '*Whatever YOU BIND on earth will be BOUND in heaven*: And, *whatever YOU LOOSE on earth will be LOOSED in heaven.*' And, again I say unto you, '*If two of you agree on earth as touching anything they ask it WILL BE DONE for them by My Father in heaven.* For, where two or three are gathered together in My name, *I am there in the midst of them.*'" "*I am with you all the days!*" *Christ being faithful to all of His promises, that is just as true today as it was in early days!* "*I am with you ALL the days!*"

Mark 16:17-18: "*These SIGNS will follow ALL who believe* [on Me]: *In My name they WILL cast out demons; they WILL speak with new tongues; they WILL take up serpents safely. If they drink any deadly thing, it WILL NOT hurt them. And, they WILL lay hands on the sick; and the sick WILL recover.*"

God cannot lie; He does not change; and Jesus Christ is the same yesterday, today and forever. That would certainly include our day. So, God wants miracles to continue today!

Luke 6:40: "The *DISCIPLE* is not above his master: But, everyone who is perfect [mature] will be just as his master." Jesus Christ is looking for *miracle-Gospel* trainees today.

John 14:12: "Truly, truly, I tell you: 'He who believes on Me, the *SAME* works I do he will do also: And greater works than these he will do, because I go to My Father [and send back the Holy Spirit to work miracles through him or her].'"

Acts 1:8: "You will receive [miracle-working] power, after the Holy Ghost has come on you: And, you will be witnesses unto Me in Jerusalem, in all Judaea, in Samaria, *AND, unto the uttermost parts of the earth.*" That not having happened yet, *believers today must fulfill that command and prophecy!*

Acts 2:38-39: "Then, Peter said to them, 'Repent, and be baptized everyone of you in the name of Jesus Christ for the remission of your sins; *THEN YOU WILL RECEIVE THE GIFT OF THE HOLY GHOST*. The promise is to you, your children, and to *ALL* who are afar off [*IN SPACE AND TIME*]; as many as the Lord our God calls." *God is still calling people today!*

First Corinthians 1:7: "You come short of no [Holy Spirit] gift while you wait for the coming of our Lord Jesus Christ": Holy Spirit gifts are meant to function until Christ returns.

First Corinthians 12:7: "The *manifestation of the Spirit is given to EVERY believer to profit.*" That is a church-wide and church-age promise. God has never rescinded it.

First Corinthians 12:28: "For, *God has SET in the church* apostles, prophets, teachers, miracles, gifts of healings, and helps, governments, diversities of tongues." *Still in effect!*

Galatians 3:2-5: "*Did you RECEIVE the Holy Spirit by the works of the law or by the hearing of faith? Are you believers that foolish? Having begun in the Spirit, are you now made* perfect by your flesh?...He Who ministers to you the Spirit, and works miracles among you, does He do it by the works of the law, or by the hearing of faith?" *Same rule for today!*

Ephesians 4:11-13: "Jesus gave [to the church] apostles, prophets, evangelists, pastors, and teachers: And all for the *perfecting of the saints*; and for the *work of ministry*, and for the *edifying of the Body of Christ: UNTIL we ALL come to the UNITY of the FAITH, and to the knowledge of the Son of God, unto a perfect man* [as individual believers, and as the Body of Christ], *unto the measure of the STATURE of the fulness of Christ."* *None of that having happened yet within the church, or by the church, is is evident we still need those ministries.*

Hebrews 2:4: "God bearing them witness both with signs and wonders, and with divers miracles, and gifts of the Holy Ghost, *according to his own will [which has never changed]."* *Even today God confirms His Gospel message with miracles for those who believe for miracles—instead of denying them!*

Malachi 3:6: "*I am the LORD; I change not*": *Which has to mean that neither His promises, nor commands, are different today than they were when they were first written!*

Hebrews 13:8: "*Jesus Christ the SAME, yesterday, today, and forever."* *That same Jesus has the same ministry today! And only the church can administer that miracle-ministry!*

James 5:14-16: "Is any sick among you? *Let him call for the elders of the church*; and let them pray over him, having anointed him with oil in the name of the Lord: The prayer of faith will save the sick one, and the Lord *WILL* raise him up; and if he has committed any sins, they will be forgiven him. *Confess your faults to one another, and pray for one another, that you may be healed.* The effectual, fervent prayer, of the righteous man [or woman] avails much." *Still true today!*

First Peter 4:10: "As every believer has received the [Holy Spirit] gift, minister it to each other *as good stewards of the manifold grace of God."* Is that command not just as binding on the church today as it was in the first century?

There is NO Scripture passage anywhere in the Bible that cancels out all or any of these in this LONG LIST of passages that make it clear that the church is both promised miracles, and actually commanded by God to believe God for miracles throughout this church-age—until Christ returns.

Our Lord clearly said in John 12:48: "He who rejects Me, and does not receive My words [which I am speaking while I am ministering here on earth], has that which judges him—the words that I have spoken will judge him in the last day." *That means exactly what our Savior said! So, if we are going to be judged on Judgment Day by the words He spoke back then, we had better heed ALL the words He spoke back then. And many of His words had to do with MIRACLES—both His promise to provide miracles throughout the entire church-age, and His command to us believers to believe Him for miracles until Jesus comes back.* I am not making up this good stuff. It is the Word of God. But, *that word has been HIDDEN from most of the modern church by private Bible interpretations of cowardly preachers, and denominational leaders. Therefore, today's church is grossly ignorant about miraculous things.*

If we individual Christians are going to be judged, based at least in part on our positive or negative response to God's promise to provide miracles, AND His command to look unto Him for miracles, then what will happen to ALL the cowardly preachers who lie on God by insisting that He no longer wills to perform miracles in our day?—Their lies being based upon their dishonest dealings with God's Written Word, the Bible!

What I just wrote may sound strange and out of place to many church-member-ears; but Jesus rebuked the Jews for rejecting miracles (Matthew 11:20-24); then prophesied that we will be judged by *ALL* of His words—which would have to include His instructions regarding miracles (John 12:48).

In the next chapter we will discuss Bible passages which tell us about God's will concerning miracles—*HOW* through Jesus Christ God made miracles possible during this entire church-age; and *WHY HE COMMANDED* believers to believe Him for miracles today. It is biblically quite simple.

Chapter Nine

At the foot of the cross and the Last Adam

In this chapter, the *"at the foot of the cross"* theology will be proven to be grossly misleading; as well as the *erroneous theological designation of the "Last Adam" as everything but the Last Adam*. Some call Him the *second Adam*, and others the *new Adam*; proving themselves to be either incompetent as Bible scholars, or *outright dishonest* in their scholarship.

I will also point out the link between the genuine biblical teaching on the cross of Christ and its vital connection with the *Last Adam*. Jesus became the *Last Adam* on the cross!

Let us begin with *the biblical teaching on the Last Adam*; then move from being at the foot of the cross, to hanging on the cross with Christ. Surely the light is already dawning on you that the *"at the foot of the cross"* theology is a falsehood. There is *NO* redemption at the foot of the cross—Only in our identifying with Christ *ON* His cross! Just hang on now.

Now, learning the real Bible teaching on the Last Adam: In 1 Corinthians 15:45, we find that Adam is called *the first man Adam*. In the Greek, it is *protos anthropos Adam*. Adam became a living soul. Genesis 2:7: "The LORD formed Adam from the dust of the ground, then *breathed into his nostrils the breath of life; and that man became a living soul.*" First Corinthians 15:45 also tells us that the *Eschatos Adam* (the Last Adam—Jesus Christ) became a life-giving Spirit.

First Corinthians 15:47 states that the *protos anthropos* (first man) was made out of dust; and then tells us that the *deuteros anthropos* (second man) was the Lord from heaven. The first made of earth; the second came from heaven. Now, Jesus Christ was never called the *second Adam*. Nor was he ever called the *new Adam*. Jesus *was designated the second man—deuteros* (second) *anthropos* (man)—never the second or new Adam. *On the cross He became everything Adam had become—sin and all its curses—achieving total redemption!*

"God has made Him [Jesus] Who did no sin *to BE SIN* for us; *that we might be made the righteousness of God IN Him* (2 Corinthians 5:21)." *The Lord actually BECOMING SIN was the primary part of His becoming the Last Adam on the cross.*

John 1:29: *"Behold the Lamb of God Who takes away the sin of the whole world."* But we must ask what made it legal for Jesus Christ to take on Him the sins of the entire world. *God does not do things haphazardly: He is obligated to PLAY by His own rules;* which He laid down at man's creation and authorization to have dominion on this earth. (I have a book telling all about God's rules governing earthly authority.)

But now let us look at more *sin-bearing* passages: Isaiah 53:4-5: "[On that cross], *CHRIST WAS WOUNDED FOR OUR TRANSGRESSIONS; BRUISED FOR OUR INIQUITIES."*

Isaiah 53:6: "The *LORD* laid on Him [Christ] *the iniquity of us all."* *That amounts to sinful Adam himself being laid on Christ on the cross,* because, as we will shortly see, *the Bible actually equates Adam with sin.* So, sin being laid on Christ was the same as Adam being laid on Christ—and that only on the cross. Jesus was the Last Adam *ONLY* on the cross!

First Peter 2:24: "Who, His own self, bore our sins in His own body on the tree, so that we, being dead to sins, should live unto righteousness." Sin described Adam, because,...

Second Corinthians 6:14-16 reveals that the lost human race is equated with sin, lawlessness, and unrighteousness. "What fellowship has righteousness with lawlessness [sin]? And what communion has light [us believers] with darkness [sinners]? *What possible agreement between Christ and the devil? And what part do we believers have with unbelievers?* [*This passage contrasts believers with unbelievers; the same as righteousness with unrighteousness, sin, or lawlessness.*] What agreement has the temple of God with idols? For, you are the temple of the Living God. As God Himself has said: 'I will dwell in them and walk among them. And I will be their God and they will be My people.'" Unbelievers are *EQUATED* with sin, lawlessness, and unrighteousness in this passage. So, when the Savior was made *TO BE SIN* on that cross (2 Corinthians 5:21) He was made *TO BE ADAM*. Yet, *since He became a life-giving Spirit, He did not remain the Last Adam.*

Look at these passages that back up what you just read. First John 3:4 states plainly: *"The one who commits sin also commits lawlessness, for sin IS lawlessness."* Sin is equated with lawlessness: And that means that sin and lawlessness are *interchangeable terms.* So *when Jesus was made TO BE SIN, He was made to be lawlessness. So says God's Word.*

First John 5:17 also says that *all unrighteousness IS sin. That makes sin and unrighteousness interchangeable terms; just like sin and lawlessness.* All three describe Adam in his fallen state—a sinner—*and even sin itself.* That has to mean that when Jesus Christ became sin on the cross He became Adam—the Last Adam; who was said to be sin, lawlessness, and unrighteousness. Those three terms describing sinners, then they have to describe Adam, the original sinner. Jesus becoming sin, then, was the same as Him becoming Adam!

For Jesus to become all sinners, He had to become Adam! But, how did Adam become all sinners? Scripturally simple! Genesis 14:20 says *Abraham gave Melchizedek a tithe of all.* And Hebrews 7:9-10 adds: "Levi, who receives tithes, *payed tithes through Abraham.* For, he, [Levi], was still in the loins [the reproductive organs] of his *great-grand-father Abraham when Melchizedek met him* [Abraham]."

This tells us that *Levi, the great-grand-son of Abraham, was inside Abraham's natural body three generations before Levi was born! That was based upon the SEED principle God built into plants, animals and people—natural* creation: That means *the entire human race was INSIDE Adam's physical body in the form of reproductive seeds. EVERY* human being came from Adam. An illustration: How many acorns may be on one oak tree? Many! But, how many oak trees are in one acorn? An unlimited number! Same with Adam.

Again, 1 Corinthians 15:45-47: *"The first man Adam was made a living soul; the last Adam [Jesus Christ] was made a life-giving Spirit. Howbeit, the spiritual came not first, but the natural;* and *afterward the spiritual.* The first man [Adam] is made of earth [chemicals]: The second man is the Lord from heaven." (Second *MAN, NOT* second Adam! *Jesus was called Adam ONLY ONCE—THE LAST ADAM—*And last means last. Moreover, Jesus did not become Adam *until He hung on the* cross. *Nor did He remain the Last Adam on and on: By His resurrection, Jesus became a life-giving Spirit. Jesus was the Last Adam for only a short time—three days and nights!)*

Now, let us go from the foot of the cross to hanging upon that cross with Christ. *Salvation was wrought ON the cross, not at the foot of it.* Remember that *Jesus did not become the Last Adam until He hung on the cross*—and redemption was purchased by Jesus becoming the Last Adam on the cross.

Romans 6:6: "Our old man [*our old self or human nature*] was crucified with Christ [on that cross], so that the body of sin might be done away." *It is our identification WITH Christ in His crucifixion* (our hanging on the cross with Him) which purchased our salvation; not our looking up at Him in great admiration from the foot of the cross. What theologian came up with that demonic idea? *And, if it is not biblical, then it is demonic.* That religious tradition originated with the devil!

No benefit purchased on the cross ever dropped from the cross, and landed at the foot of it. There are no shortcuts to receiving salvation! *The Apostle Paul never preached any.* He emphasized our having been crucified with Christ upon His cross. There is no biblical "at the foot of the cross" doctrine!

Instead, Paul boldly said: "We preach Christ crucified; to the Jews a stumbling block and to Gentiles foolishness; but to us who are called, *from both Jews and Gentiles*, Christ is both the power of God and the wisdom of God: Because, the foolishness of God is wiser than men, and the weakness of God is stronger than men (1 Corinthians 1:23)." The literal Greek is *having been crucified*—Jesus is not still hanging on the cross. *He was raised up from the dead. And, by faith we were both crucified with Him, and raised up with Him* (in our inner man—our *SPIRIT* has been resurrected with Christ!)

Another crucifixion passage is 1 Corinthians 2:2: "I [Paul] determined to not know anything among you, except Christ, and Him having been crucified." *And that crucifixion doctrine included our identification WITH Christ in His crucifixion; not our admiring His cross-sufferings from beneath the cross.*

Just how real was that Bible Reality to Paul? Galatians 2:20-21 tells us: "*I have been crucified WITH Christ: So, it is no longer I who live, but Christ lives in me; and the life I now live in the flesh I live by the faith of the Son of God.*" (*REAL!*)

Galatians 6:14: "God forbid that I should boast except in the cross of Christ—*by Whom the world was crucified to me, and I to the world.*" *Our being identified with Jesus Christ in His crucifixion saves us from our former lifestyle of sin, and brings us into a new lifestyle of right-living*: "If any man is in Christ he is a *NEW* creature; *OLD* things have passed away, and *ALL* things have become *NEW*; and *ALL* the *NEW* things are of God (2 Corinthians 5:17-18)." And check this out:

Galatians 3:27: "All of you who were baptized into Christ have put on Christ [in the Greek, have clothed yourself with Christ]": *Referring not to water-baptism, but to baptism into the Body of Christ BY the Holy Spirit* (1 Corinthians 12:13). That is our identification with Christ. And in addition,...

Galatians 5:24: "All of those who belong to Christ *HAVE CRUCIFIED* the flesh with all its passions and desires." How so? *By identifying with Jesus Christ! Accepting Jesus Christ as Savior means our acceptance of all that He accomplished for us in His crucifixion*: Because, *when He became Adam on the cross He became US on the cross! And by His bearing all the bad stuff that we had incurred by our identification with that first Adam, we inherit all of the good stuff Christ bought for us by Him becoming the Last Adam—and suffering all the bad stuff connected to the first Adam.* Go over that again!

That Church of Christ author called Jesus both the *New* Adam and the *Second* Adam; and did not even explain what he meant by that—*proving that he is incompetent as a Bible teacher.* That is just one of *MANY* flaws in Church of Christ doctrine. Their entire doctrinal system is a religious farce.

In the next chapter we will look into how our redemption was achieved by the Last Adam. When Jesus Christ became the Last Adam, He became all that Adam had become in his fall in the Garden of Eden. *He bore not only Adam's sin, and our sins, but also all the curses attached to Adam's sin, and our sins.* That is the good news of the Gospel message!

Chapter Ten

Taking on the first Adam and his problems

The *primary problem* of the first Adam (and, therefore, of all the rest of us human beings) was pointed out in Romans 5:12, which clearly states: "By *ONE MAN* [Adam] sin entered into this world, and death came by [or with the] sin; and so, death passed upon all men, because all have sinned." Thus, Adam taking on an entirely *NEW* nature—sinful nature—by agreeing with, and obeying, Satan's words—and disagreeing with, and disobeying, God's Words—*Adam's offspring would also be strapped with the very same sinful nature—which by nature rebels against God. Because of that SEED PRINCIPLE which God built into mankind* (same as plants and animals), *Adam's SIN NATURE surfaces in generation after generation since Adam fell.* Every human being inherits that very same sin nature—lodged within every lost human spirit.

Sin being humanity's primary problem, then SIN was the primary problem the Word-of-God-made-flesh had to take on Himself and solve. But remember that sin opened the door to death—and death is a broad term that includes every other human problem. Thus every human problem SHORT of death is itself A DEGREE OF DEATH. So, in bearing our sins, Jesus bore all of those other evil conditions connected to sin—as we will see later in the chapter. But to the sin condition first.

Second Corinthians 5:21 starts us down that Bible path: "God has made Him [Jesus] Who knew no [never committed any] sin *TO* [actually] *BE SIN* for us; that we might [actually] *BECOME THE RIGHTEOUSNESS OF GOD IN HIM* [Christ]." Jesus never sinned. However, on the cross He was made *TO BE* sin. Adam and all his offspring being equated with sin (2 Corinthians 6:14-16), *when Jesus was MADE TO BE SIN on the cross, He became ADAM AND US on the cross—becoming SIN, ADAM AND US ONLY ONCE, and ONLY ON THE CROSS. He was the Last Adam one time—on the cross and in Hades!*

John 1:29: "Behold, the Lamb of God [Jesus], Who takes away the sin of *the whole world.*" Now, *that is A LOT OF SIN!* Moreover, think about *all of the different kinds of gross sins.* Christ became all of that! If not, then these Scriptures have no meaning. *What a PRICE was PAID for our redemption!*

Christ BORE the brunt of God's punishment for every sin. Isaiah 53:5: "*Jesus was WOUNDED for OUR transgressions; BRUISED for OUR iniquities.*" That happened on the cross.

Isaiah 53:6: "*The LORD HAS LAID ON HIM* [Jesus Christ] *the iniquity of us all.*" *Sinners being EQUATED with sin itself,* according to 2 Corinthians 6:14-16, *when God laid our sins upon Christ, He laid us on Him; because of our connection to Adam. Christ was the Last Adam and us on that cross. How else could we have been crucified WITH HIM* (Romans 6:6)? If we were *WITH* Him, then we were *WITH* Him!

First Peter 2:24: "Who, His own self, bore our sins in His own body on the tree, so that we, being dead to sins, should live unto righteousness." Agreeing with 2 Corinthians 5:21.

Hebrews 2:9: "That He, by the grace of God, should taste [spiritual] death for every man." Throughout history all men have died physically, so the death that Christ tasted on the cross, and in Hades, *had to be spiritual death.* And, *spiritual death is the parent of physical death.* In Genesis 2:17, Adam was warned: "*On the day you eat of the tree of knowledge of good and evil you will SURELY die.* In the literal Hebrew it is "*dying you will die." On the day Adam ate the forbidden fruit HIS SPIRIT DIED. He was separated from God. That is what spiritual death is.* Adam died physically nine-hundred-thirty years later. Also consider these other informative passages:

Ephesians 2:1: "God has made alive, you who were *dead in trespasses and sins* [while you were sinners]." Ephesians 2:5: "When we were dead in trespasses, God made us alive, together with Christ." Colossians 2:13: "And you being dead in your trespasses and the uncircumcision of your flesh, He has made alive, together with Christ; having forgiven you all trespasses." First Timothy 5:6: "Widows, [who vow to live for Christ alone, but break their vows, in order to marry] live in pleasure, and are *dead while they live.*" The walking dead!

Second Corinthians 5:14 says that: "If One [Christ] died for all [*every person on this planet*], then [in Christ] all died." As far as God is concerned man's *primary problem* has been solved in Christ. First Timothy 4:10 explains it clearly: "The Living God is the Savior of *ALL* men, especially of those who believe [for salvation]." *God has provided salvation for every person on earth through Christ—but ONLY those who believe for the salvation, which Christ wrought for them on the cross, will receive that salvation, which Christ wrought for them on the cross.* "God was in Christ, *RECONCILING the* [entire lost] *world to Himself* (2 Corinthians 5:19)." But, *only those who truly repent, and put their trust in the Gospel message, are saved.* Salvation is available to all, but it is not automatic.

Romans 6:6: "*Our OLD sinful human nature was crucified WITH the Christ, so that our body of sin might be done away with.*" Identified with Christ in His crucifixion, death, burial and resurrection. He identified with us on the cross to save us, and we must identify with Him on the cross to be saved.

Galatians 5:24 puts that *Gospel reality* in a nutshell: "*All of those who belong to Christ have crucified the flesh with its passions and desires.*" And we believers do belong to Christ! First Corinthians 6:19-20: "Do you not know that your body is the temple of the Holy Spirit, Who lives inside you, Whom you have [as a gift] from God, and that *YOU ARE NOT YOUR OWN?* For you were bought for a price; therefore glorify God in your body, and in your spirit, which belong to God." And, "You were bought at a price; so do not become the slaves of men (1 Corinthians 7:23)." We believers are God's property! Believers are even identified with Christ in His ascension to heaven, because we have been *seated with Him in heavenly places*, according to Ephesians 2:6. (How did we get there?)

Moreover: "You who have been baptized into Christ have 'put on' Christ (Galatians 3:27)." Those words rendered "put on" mean "to clothe oneself with." *That means we Christians are now WEARING Christ.* And, we were baptized into Christ *BY* the Holy Spirit, *NOT BY* water-baptism. We are told that in 1 Corinthians 12:13. The believer's body being immersed in water—the chemical substance known as $H2O$—does not join the believer's spirit to Christ. *That can be accomplished only by the Holy Spirit regenerating our spirit.*

We must remember that *spiritual death* is the root-cause of *every EVIL physical condition*. So, *when Christ addressed our spiritual-death condition on the cross, He also took on all those other evil conditions*. Consider these Scriptures, which clearly reveal that, *when Christ took on Himself our spiritual problems on the cross, He at the same time bore our physical and financial problems*. But, Church of Christ preachers, as well as preachers of most denominations today, continue to cheat their church members out of Christ's cross-solutions to both their physical ailments and financial short-falls!

Galatians 3:13: "Christ has redeemed us from the curse of the law [*ALL* of it], being *MADE A CURSE* for us: For, *just as it is written, cursed is everyone who hangs on a tree*." See Deuteronomy 21:23. Upon that cross, Christ was *MADE TO BE A CURSE* just as He was *MADE TO BE SIN*—Same place, same time! He redeemed us from the curse of the law. What were the curses of the law? Deuteronomy 28:15 informs us: "If you do not hearken to the voice of the *LORD* your God, to observe all of His commands and all of His statutes, *then all these different curses will come upon you and overtake you*." In following verses, *many different diseases and other bodily infirmities are mentioned by name*. Deuteronomy 28:61 also warns: "*Every sickness and every plague NOT written in this Book of the Law will the LORD bring upon you, until you are destroyed*." *That means that EVERY sickness is a curse*. And Jesus Christ redeemed us from the sickness curse—all of it!

Isaiah 53:4-5: "Surely, He has *borne our sicknesses* and *carried our pains*: Yet, we esteemed Him stricken, smitten of God, and afflicted [for His own sins]...And, *the chastisement which purchased OUR Shaaloom*—wholeness, completeness, well-being, peace, and prosperity—was upon Christ: And by His *BRUISE* [*singular*] we are healed." The Hebrew in Isaiah 53:5, and the Greek in 1 Peter 2:24, are *singular, not plural: What the Bible authors communicated is vastly different from what most preachers stick with today*—stripes—plural—*the reverse of Bible Truth. They insist that the stripes the Roman soldiers laid on Christ's back HEALED US*. However, *there is NO CONNECTION between those NATURAL whip lashes and SUPERNATURAL HEALING COMING FROM GOD!*

Isaiah 53:10 reveals the true source of divine healing: "It pleased the *LORD* [Jehovah-Rapha] *TO BRUISE* Him: He has made Him sick [literally, crushed Him with disease—ours]." Men did whip the Lord before his crucifixion, but how could that touch a problem with spiritual roots? *It was what God Himself did to Christ ON THE CROSS, NOT WHAT MEN DID TO HIM BEFORE THE CROSS, that healed us!*

Matthew 8:16-17 *proves that Isaiah was prophesying the supernatural healing of PHYSICAL sickness and disease, not spiritual infirmity: "They brought unto Jesus many who were demon-possessed: And He cast out those evil spirits with His word, and healed all who were physically sick: That it might be fulfilled which was spoken by Isaiah the prophet, saying, 'Himself took our infirmities, and bore our sicknesses.'"*

First Peter 2:24: "By Whose [Christ's] *wound* [*singular in the Greek*] you were healed." *That would be the wound that GOD inflicted on Jesus on the cross.* The first part of 1 Peter 2:24 says that Jesus bore our sins on the *TREE*. Then Peter said that by His bruise (which He suffered at God's hand on that very same tree—the cross), we were healed. Let God be true, but every contradictory preacher a liar (Romans 3:4).

The curse of the law also included poverty. Deuteronomy 28:47-48: "Because you served not the *LORD* your God with joyfulness, and with gladness of heart, for the abundance of all things [God's divine provisions]; then you will serve your enemies, which the *LORD* will *SEND* against you, in hunger, in thirst, in nakedness, and in the want [lack] of all things." The Bible says *POVERTY IS A CURSE*, and Christ redeemed us from the curse of poverty by Himself *BECOMING* a curse upon that cross. The Bible is true; religious doctrine the lie. *Will we believe men's lies, or God's unchanging Bible Truth?*

DEBT is one more form of poverty. Deuteronomy 28:44: "[*If you do not obey all of My commands*], strangers will lend to you, but you will not lend to them [you being broke]."

And now look at 2 Corinthians 8:9: "You know the grace of our Lord Jesus Christ, that, although He was rich, yet for your sakes He became poor [only on that cross], so that you through His poverty [on that cross] might be made rich."

In Matthew 26:11, Jesus Christ said: "You have the poor with you always, but Me you do not have always." That was before He went to the cross. Thus, our Lord said out of His own mouth that He was *NOT POOR* prior to His crucifixion.

Second Corinthians 8:9 tells us plainly that He was rich, but that *He BECAME POOR at some point in time.* Christ fed the multitudes, had a treasurer, gave to the poor, and never lacked anything during His earthly ministry. So, He was not poor until He hung upon the cross; *where He bore all of our problems—including financial and material lack.*

Isaiah 53:12 at least hints that *Christ took upon Himself our poverty while He was on the cross, and then shared with us the spoils of that war—everything He purchased for us on that tree*: "He will divide the *SPOIL* with the strong [in faith]; because, He poured out His soul unto death."

Our Savior purchased even *MORE* blessings for us while He was on the cross, and we will discuss all those blessings as well. And in that process, we will continue to expose and refute even more erroneous Church of Christ doctrines.

The scriptural revelation we have covered in this chapter *lays the foundation* for the biblical realities appearing on the following pages. Much eye-opening revelation on the way!

Chapter Eleven

Why Church of Christ doctrine comes up short—A

The Church of Christ preachers (*just as the preachers in many other denominations—to be fair*) build their theological doctrines upon the wrong foundation. All of them teach that the main purposes of Holy Spirit gifts and ministries in the first century were *to get those New Testament books written, and to establish the church.* Therefore, *they all come short of perceiving God's long range plan for both the church and the world.* This chapter and the next reveal how they miss it in both the *practical* realm and the *scriptural* realm.

On the practical side of the issue: During Old Testament times, God's miracles were performed more to deliver people than to get the Old Testament books written. God's purpose through Jesus Christ was basically the same—to get people delivered from Satan's debilitating works. And, *even though some miracles were recorded in some New Testament books, those miracles recorded had nothing to do with writing those books.* And, *what about all the miracles that occurred AFTER the New Testament books were written? They were obviously performed to deliver hurting people; not to get books penned, or to get the church established once for all.*

After the first century was over, and after the LAST NEW TESTAMENT BOOK had been written, the very same kinds of miracles continued to manifest, both within, and through, the church—even into the fourth century. The next generation of believers testified about the miracles occurring in their day; and so did following generations. In the first five volumes of the "Church Fathers" writings, we find *multiple references to the same kinds of MIRACLES that were recorded in many of the New Testament books.* Some of those writers were *Justin Martyr, Irenaeus, Tertullian, Cyprian,* and *Origen.* Their lives ranged from the second to the fourth centuries. If you have access to those early church writings, you will want to look up pages 190, 240, 243, 409, and 531 in volume one; pages

188 and 447 in volume 3; pages 473 and 614 in volume 4; and page 290 in volume 5. Just as in the Gospels and Acts, people got *healed of serious illnesses, demons were cast out,* and even some *dead were raised*. And, not only did men in those days perform such miracles, but women as well. And, even children exercised some of those supernatural gifts. *So the argument that miracles in the first century were primarily for getting the church established once for all is an excuse to not believe miracles are for today.* Anyway, the church HAS TO BE REESTABLISHED IN EVERY GENERATION! And, if it took miracles to do that back then, the same is true today.

And, if one of God's purposes for the twelve apostles was writing the New Testament, why did only three of the twelve write a New Testament book? *Peter, John and Matthew were the only ones of the twelve original apostles who penned any New Testament work.* All of the other New Testament books were written by men who were *not of the twelve*. That within itself destroys that hypocritical Church of Christ doctrine.

Those other books were written by Mark, Luke, the Lord's half-brother James, His other half-brother Jude and Paul. So one more Church of Christ doctrine *bites the dust*. And yet, those preachers hold onto that false doctrine as though any denial of it would be a denial of all biblical truth. As it turns out, those preachers are the biblical-truth-deniers!

What biblical truth are we talking about here? *The truth which is plainly written in the Bible for all to see and believe! The theological arguments of the highly-educated theologians in the Church of Christ are based on theological speculation; not actual biblical teaching.* A prime premise within Church of Christ doctrine is: *Where the Bible is silent we are silent: Where the Bible speaks we speak. The Bible says absolutely nothing about miracles being TEMPORARY; or that they were performed ONLY by those twelve apostles; or that they were performed primarily to ESTABLISH the church on this planet.* So, *the Church of Christ does speak where the Bible is silent; contrary to their claims. And, they remain silent about issues the Bible is not silent about.* Therefore, the Church of Christ *LIES* from *BOTH* doctrinal directions. So why trust anything preachers in that religious group try to push on people?

Holy Scripture instructs us about God's will concerning miracles. Consider this primary scriptural reality—miracles were *embedded* in Christ's sacrifice. And, since His sacrifice was permanent, *whatever is embedded in His sacrifice must also be permanent!* Hebrews 9:12 informs us that: *"Not with the blood of goats, and calves, but with His own blood Christ entered The Most Holy Place* [up in heaven] *once and for all, having obtained eternal redemption."* Nothing about Christ's blood, *or about what His blood accomplished*, was temporal. Thus, whatever God's Word says is included in the sacrifice, which Christ made on that cross, will always be available to every person who believes. In Luke 22:20, Jesus said: *"This cup is the New Covenant in My blood, which is shed for you." That means that EVERY blessing Jesus purchased for us on the cross is still IN His shed blood, which He deposited upon that heavenly altar—and, therefore, CANNOT BE TAMPERED WITH—NOR DIMINISHED IN ITS REDEMPTIVE POWER.* Luke 22:20 proves without doubt that *the entire New Covenant is embedded in the shed blood of Jesus Christ*; deposited up in heaven. And it cannot be touched, either by angels, or men: And especially not by the devil. Matthew and Mark recorded the same about *the New Covenant being in Christ's blood.*

How can any preacher conscientiously claim that certain parts of Christ's sacrifice would fade over time? Theologians who promote such blasphemy *are dishonest with Scripture, with the people they minister to, and even with God Himself! And being dishonest regarding Bible Truth certainly proves a preacher incompetent—disqualifying him or her from Gospel ministry.* Claiming that God *PLANNED* that miracles were to cease *AFTER* the first century brands those theologians the church's *ENEMIES*; and *NOT* the church's friends. And, *that problem is much more SERIOUS than the majority of church members realize today. EVERY Christian needs to know that God not only WANTS miracles to happen UNTIL the return of Christ; but even commanded such!* Ponder Matthew 28:20.

Let us look in depth at some of the blessings Jesus Christ wrought for us upon the cross by His shed blood and broken body—blessings most Church of Christ theologians are either silent about; or actually outspoken against!

Second Corinthians 5:21 says that: *"God MADE Christ, Who committed no sin, TO BE SIN for us; that we MIGHT BE MADE the righteousness of God in Him."* "Now, *the Church of Christ teaches the forgiveness of sins, do they not?"* They do indeed! *But only the forgiveness of sins.* Yet, the Greek word rendered forgiveness also means *remission*—which actually means the *removal* of sins. John 1:29: "Behold, the Lamb of God Who *takes away* the sin of the world." And the removal of our sins does not leave us mere blanks. Christ was made to be sin so that we might be made righteous—*And with the very righteousness of God! Such did not appear in that 400+ page monstrosity written by that Church of Christ theologian. Christians are not living in some kind of theological no-man's land—merely forgiven of our past sins. We who are IN Christ BY the NEW BIRTH have actually become NEW CREATURES* (2 Corinthians 5:17)—*Which is a lot bigger blessing than the mere forgiveness of sins!* As a matter of fact, in 1 John 4:17, John said: "As He [Jesus Christ] is, so are we in this world." *Jesus Christ is not just a sinner who has been forgiven!* That Church of Christ theologian did mention 1 John 4:17 in his book; but instead of pointing out: "As Jesus is, so are we in this world right *NOW*," he emphasized the part of that verse which promises that believers will have *boldness on the day of judgment*. The man failed to focus upon God's promise of miracles in our new life. He only stressed that believers are to *LIVE A MORALLY DIFFERENT KIND OF LIFE. NO* mention of what Jesus did for our health, finances, etc. Eventually, I must point out his shortcomings in those areas as well, but first let me finish that sin scene. Isaiah 53:4-5: "Christ was wounded for *OUR* transgressions; and was bruised for *OUR* iniquities." Isaiah 53:6: "The *LORD* [Jehovah] has laid upon Him [the Lord Jesus] the iniquity of us all." Finally, 1 Peter 2:24: "Who, His own self bore *OUR* sins in *HIS* own body on the tree [cross], that we [who are in Christ], being dead unto sins, should live unto righteousness..."

Now who could deny that the blessing of deliverance from sin is EMBEDDED in the shed blood of Jesus Christ; which is deposited up in heaven? But, in that same sacrifice, He Who took our sins upon Himself also took all of our other human problems upon Himself, in order to deliver us from them all!

Thus, those blessings have to be *EMBEDDED* in Christ's sacrifice as well. *The same person*—Jesus Christ—*made the same sacrifice at the very same place*—the cross—*and at the same time*—while He was on the cross. Thus, whatever God placed on Jesus while He was hanging on that cross was for the same purpose—*to get those evil things off our backs and out of our lives.* To deny that truth is to deny the Scriptures, which CLEARLY REVEAL that truth. Who gave preachers the right to choose what they WANT TO BELIEVE AND PREACH, and what they DO NOT WANT TO BELIEVE AND PREACH?

Galatians 3:13: "Jesus Christ has redeemed us from the curse of the law [*every curse which is under the law*], having *BECOME* a curse for us: For, cursed is everyone who hangs upon a tree [the cross]." See Deuteronomy 21:23. *Sin is not the curse, but the CAUSE of the curse.* Thus, the curse is not sin, but the end-result of sin. So, sin and the curse are *NOT* the same. Yet they are closely connected; for sin opened the door to all the curses—sickness, poverty, etc., etc. Also,...

That word "*REDEEMED*," in Galatians 3:13, is actually a financial term meaning "*to BUY up ALL there is to buy*." And that means on the cross Jesus became everything God says is a curse—buying our total freedom from every curse. That curse-list is recorded in Deuteronomy 28:15-68. *Christ paid the FULL price for our deliverance from EVERY CURSE.* But 1 Corinthians 6:19-20 also says that "*We are not our own. We too were BOUGHT for a price: Thus, we are to glorify God in our body, and in our spirit; both of which BELONG to God in Christ.*" It should be obvious that, *if sin in our spirit does not glorify God, neither does sickness in our body glorify God!*

The curse of the law includes physical sickness, poverty, and other human calamities listed in Deuteronomy chapter twenty-eight. And, *the Son of God became every one of those curses on the cross—because God put every one of them on Him as He hung on the cross—redeeming us from them all!*

Scriptural case in point: "You know the grace of our Lord Jesus Christ, that, although He was rich, *yet for your sakes He became poor* [on the cross], that you through His poverty might be rich (2 Corinthians 8:9)." *Christ was not poor until He hung upon the cross*, because he said plainly in Matthew 26:11: "You have the poor with you always—*BUT* Me you do not have always." Our Lord was not poor before He became poor upon the cross. At what other time could He have been poor, since *He said He was not poor prior to His crucifixion?* When Jesus was just a baby, kings brought Him the world's riches. In His ministry, Jesus fed multitudes. He even had a treasurer, who stole money from the money box. Christ was not poor *UNTIL* His Father *CURSED* Him with poverty—our poverty—while He was on the cross—in order to redeem us from poverty. End of all absurd religious arguments!

Isaiah 53:4-5 tells us plainly that, *Jesus Christ bore our diseases and carried our pains*. Moreover, the *chastisement or punishment that purchased our peace—Hebrew sheeloom*: Which means *wholeness, completeness, physical health* and *financial and material prosperity—was upon Him—and with His BRUISE we are healed.* (Bruise is singular, not plural.)

Thus, just as God laid all of our iniquities upon Jesus as He hung upon the cross, He placed all of our diseases upon Him—in the same place, and at the same time. Isaiah 53:10 tells us plainly that "*It pleased the LORD to BRUISE Him. He [crushed] Him with [our] sickness.*" In Christ's sacrifice, our diseases were removed just like our sins were removed. And Matthew 8:16-17 confirms it: "*He healed all the sick to fulfill Isaiah's prophecy that says: 'Himself took our infirmities and bore our sicknesses.'*" First Peter 2:24 *ECHOES* Isaiah 53:5: "*By His wound* [singular, not plural] *you were healed.*" (The cross-wound God inflicted on Jesus *HEALED* our wounds.)

The next chapter adds to the long list of *cross-purchased blessings*, which obviously belong to us believers, but which just happen to be missing from the Church of Christ gospel. Moreover, we will discuss the crux of this important matter; which is God's plainly-expressed will in that miracle-matter. We will continue presenting the redemption truth, for which this chapter has laid the biblical foundation.

Chapter Twelve

Why Church of Christ doctrine comes up short—B

This chapter deals with three obvious truths which "JUST HAPPEN TO BE MISSING" from Church of Christ teachings: Number one—*upon that cross, Jesus Christ purchased for us even MORE blessings than those I pointed out in the previous chapter* (And, even some of the benefits I already mentioned are not found in Church of Christ theology.). Number two— *Every human problem Christ encountered and solved in both His ministry and sacrifice continue to plague the human race in EACH AND EVERY GENERATION.* And number three—*the redemptive names of God testify not only to what God does, but to WHO He is—His unchanging character!* Therefore, His miracle-working personality remaining *THE SAME* (according to Malachi 3:6), *God wants His miracles to continue!* Church of Christ theologians, and other preachers too, will not allow God to be Himself in their theology—CHEATING their church members, ALL the lost, and even God Himself! How does one cheat God? By not accepting *ALL* the blessings He provided by Christ's *COSTLY* sacrifice. *It is like a slap in their faces!*

The first purpose first—Additional cross-bought benefits: *MORE* than sins forgiven, hell avoided, diseases healed, and financial problems conquered, our Savior addressed on the cross *ALL* other conditions that *harass* the human race.

The very fact that these additional *cross-benefits* that we will cover in this chapter are missing from Church of Christ theology reveals either the *dishonesty of their theologians, or their lack of biblical knowledge—either of which disqualifies them as Bible teachers.* Likely it is both *dishonesty* and *poor scholarship. Jesus Christ dealt with EVERY human condition while hanging upon that cross—because He was obligated to pay for ALL the blessings He had administered to the hurting people during His ministry.* That is a *Bible Truth* that cannot lightly be dismissed—although the Church of Christ does.

Since on that cross Christ paid for ALL of those blessings He had blessed people with BEFORE He hung on the cross, then those very same blessings must STILL be available for everyone on this side of the cross who believes God for them. The price *HAVING BEEN PAID, ONCE FOR ALL,* the benefits that have been paid for *must continue to be available to ALL who believe. Cross-benefits are attached to the PRICE Jesus paid, NOT to people who lived in the first century.* Looking at those additional cross-blessings, a primary one is...

EVERY human problem stems from man's connection to the devil; *so that was a major issue the Lord had to address while upon the cross.* John 8:44: "You are of your [spiritual] father, the devil. So the desires of your [spiritual] father you also *WILL* to do. He was a murderer from the very beginning [of his career as God's archenemy], and *does NOT remain in the truth, BECAUSE THERE IS NO TRUTH IN HIM.* When the devil tells a lie he speaks from his own resources, *for he is a liar, and the father of both lies and liars.*" The entire human race outside of Christ gets its *NATURE* from the devil. *Lying and murdering are common traits of the fallen human race.* It has been that way since Adam's fall in the Garden of Eden. See Romans 1:18-32. *It actually describes modern society!*

Since all other human problems sprang from fallen man being the *spiritual offspring* of the devil himself (John 8:44), then *our Lord certainly had to take on that human condition while on the cross—on which He addressed all other human ailments as well.* How did He do it? Let Scripture explain.

Genesis 3:15: "I, [God,] will put enmity between you [the devil] and the woman, and between your seed and her Seed [Christ—Gal. 3:16]; He will bruise your head, and you will bruise His heel." *Enmity being between the devil and man in EVERY compartment of human life, then Jesus Christ had to redeem ALL compartments of human life!* Can you see that?

Every human problem was encountered by Jesus Christ on the cross; including our main problem—*our identification with the devil, through our identification with Adam, through Adam's identification with the devil.* Three Bible witnesses:

John 3:14: "As Moses lifted up the *serpent* on a pole out in the wilderness [long ago], *so must the Son of man be lifted up* [on a cross]." *Thus the connection between Jesus Christ's sacrifice on the cross and mankind's devil-problem.* And still another scriptural witness to man's devil-connection,...

Our Savior, referring to His upcoming cross-experience, said in John 12:31-33: "*'NOW is the judgment of this world* [order, ruled by the devil—2 Corinthians 4:4 and Ephesians 2:2—the god of this age is the spirit that works in this fallen world system]. *Now the ruler of this world* [the devil] *will be cast out.* [Do you see the connection?] And I, [Jesus Christ], if I am lifted up from earth [on a cross] will draw all men to Myself.' Jesus said that, signifying by what death He would die [by crucifixion]." And a third witness,...

Hebrews 2:14 gives us more *LIGHT* on the subject. "That through death [His death upon the cross], He [Christ] might *destroy* [*render ineffective*] him who had the power of death; the devil." By means of His death on the cross, *Jesus Christ separated Christians from the devil*—one of our most needed benefits *NOT* found in Church of Christ theology. And, that *scriptural truth EXPLAINS* many other *scriptural truths*. *The devil being involved in every human problem, then to save us from all those other human problems, Christ was obligated to take on mankind's devil-connection problem in the process.* It was all solved by Christ's one sacrifice on the cross.

One *problem* attached to man's *devil-connection-problem* was mankind's *Hell-problem.* Even though Church of Christ theology *does cover that problem*, and Christ's *cross-solution of it*—to a certain extent—their doctrinal works provide little Bible proof of that vital Bible Truth: Another flaw of Church of Christ theology. Consider the following Scriptures, which reveal the *PRICE* that Jesus Christ paid to save us from the Hell-problem. God's Word produces genuine confidence that our deliverance from Hell has been secured by our Savior.

That big thick Church of Christ doctrine book I read has both a subject index and a Scripture index in the back; and within the subject index *the word HELL does not appear one time*. I did find in that Scripture index those five Scriptures below, but in all five references, the author only used them to make the connection between Christ and King David. *NO MENTION OF HELL in any of them!* Here are those passages:

As though Jesus Himself were speaking, Psalms 16:9-10 says: "Therefore, My heart is glad, and My glory rejoices; My flesh also will rest in hope. For, *You will not leave My soul in Sheol* [The Old Testament word for Hell: The New Testament word for Hell is Hades.]: *Nor will You allow Your Holy One to see corruption* [*DECAY of the BODY*]." That Church of Christ author mentioned *NONE* of this in his comments upon this Scripture passage. Moreover, the *SUBTITLE* of that book is: "*A BIBLICAL ECCLESIOLOGY FOR TODAY.*" Ecclesiology has to do with the Gospel message about our Savior's sacrifice, which includes our deliverance from Hell. The price He paid for that Gospel-benefit was His suffering *HELL* in our place. Jesus suffered everything Adam was due; including Hell.

Matthew 12:40: "For as Jonah was three days and three nights in the belly of that *big fish, so will the Son of Man be three days and three nights in the HEART of the earth.*" Now, heart means the center. *The Spirit of Jesus Christ was in the very center of this terrestrial ball for three days and nights, while His DEAD body lay just beneath its surface.*

Acts 2:24: "God raised the Lord up, having loosed [put a stop to] the *pains of death*, because it was not possible that He [Jesus Christ] should be held [prisoner] by it [*referring to the pains of spiritual death*]." *Dead bodies suffer no pain. So, death-pains had to refer to Christ's spiritual suffering in Hell.*

Acts 2:27: "You [God] will not leave My [Jesus Christ's] *SOUL* in Hell. Neither will You allow Your Holy One [Christ] to see *corruption* [*no bodily decay*]." The Lord's *SOUL*, was in Hell, not His fleshly body. The word rendered Hell *here, and elsewhere in the New Testament*, is the Greek word "Hades." Hades is *NOT* the grave! *That Church of Christ author taught that HADES is the grave*—One more Church of Christ error. Our Lord's *BODY* lay dead in the grave, while His *SOUL* was incarcerated in Hell for three days and nights.

Again in Acts 2:31: "David seeing this in prophecy spoke about the resurrection of Christ—that His soul was not left down in Hell [*Hades—underworld abode of departed spirits*], nor did His flesh [body] see [experience] corruption [decay]."

What business did our Lord have down in Hades? It was actually our business He was taking care of. Hell was part of mankind's payment for sin, *and Jesus took on Himself both our sin and the payment for sin.* Just one more cross-benefit Church of Christ theology falls short on teaching about.

One more witness about all this is 1 Peter 3:18-20: "For Christ also suffered once [on the cross, and down in Hades] for our sins—the just [Jesus Christ] for the unjust [sinners], that He might bring us unto God; being put to death in the flesh, but made alive [*IN* His Spirit, which was *IN* Hades] by the Holy Spirit: By Whom also He went and preached to the spirits in prison [down in Hades]—people who formerly were disobedient [to God's Word preached by Noah—2 Peter 2:5], when the Divine long-suffering waited in the days of *NOAH*, while the ark was being prepared; in which only a few, eight souls, were saved through water." *Christ's born-again Spirit, NOT HIS BODY, which yet lay lifeless in the grave, went and preached to those spirits in that underworld prison.* And that was an "I told you so" message; *NOT giving them a SECOND CHANCE to be saved. There is no second chance after death.*

Another redemption-blessing the Savior *PAID FOR* in His sacrifice: *On one side of that REDEMPTION coin, so to speak, was our separation from the devil, and on the other side was our being reconciled to God;* and *His promise to NEVER leave us nor FORSAKE us.* Scriptures for those benefits:

Second Corinthians 5:19: "God the Father was in Christ, reconciling the [entire lost] world unto Himself [through the cross]." And, one result of our being reconciled to God,...

Hebrews 13:5: "Your lifestyle [in Christ] must be without covetousness; and you must be content with the things you have: Because, [God] has [promised]: 'I will never leave you, nor forsake you.'" *An extreme price was paid for that benefit!*

Scripture revealing that cross-payment—Matthew 27:46: "About the ninth hour [three o'clock in the afternoon] Jesus cried with a loud voice, saying: 'Eli, Eli, lama sabachthani?' which was to say, 'My God, My God, why have You forsaken Me?'" Everything Christ suffered on the cross was payment for some blessing the human race was desperate for!

More biblical proof of that cross-payment: Romans 5:10: "When we were [God's] enemies [*because THE DEVIL himself was our spiritual father*], we were reconciled to God through the death of His Son." Because of that payment Jesus made on the cross, and in Hell, "God has made us accepted in the Beloved [Christ Himself] (Ephesians 1:6)."

One more cross-blessing related to our deliverance from the devil, and our reconciliation to God, is found in Romans 8:31-35: "What, then, should we say to these things? *If God is for us, who then can be against us?* He Who did not spare His very own Son, *BUT* delivered Him up for us all [in order to purchase our total deliverance], how will He not with Him also freely give us all things [which He purchased for us on the cross]? [Therefore,] who will bring an accusation against God's elect? It is God Who justifies us [so He will not accuse us]. Who is he who will condemn us? [Not Christ, because,] it is Christ Who died and has risen, and Who is even now at the right hand of God making intercession for us [instead of condemning us]. Who will separate us from the love of God, and of Jesus Christ? Will tribulation, distress, persecution, famine, nakedness, peril or sword?" No! Because, in Christ, believers have power to overcome all of that (Romans 8:37).

The second REASON miracles have continued throughout the past two millennia, down to the PRESENT day (whenever and wherever people have believed God for miracles) is that, *people in every generation have continued to have the same physical needs Christ ministered to during His time on earth, and addressed in His sacrifice on the cross.* Thus, *that same need for healing-miracles continues down to the present day; and will continue to do so, until the end of this evil age.* Such being a practical reason for miracles to continue in our day, there is no need to appeal to Scripture for proof of that.

A third undeniable proof that miracles were intended by God Himself to continue throughout this present evil age is: *God's personality is perpetual. His own redemptive titles are themselves sufficient proof of that scriptural truth!* So, let us investigate *that Bible Truth; which is missing from Church of Christ theology.* If they believed and taught these great Bible Truths, they would not believe and teach the many lies they push on their own church members and everybody else.

The name JEHOVAH is combined with several redemptive titles which reveal not only God's REDEMPTIVE ACTIVITIES, but also His REDEMPTIVE CHARACTER. We will first look at what the term *JEHOVAH* itself signifies.

The name *JEHOVAH* basically means the *ETERNAL ONE*, the *SELF-EXISTENT ONE*, and the *IMMUTABLE ONE*—Which obviously proves that *JEHOVAH GOD* does not, and indeed cannot, change—but instead *remains the same from eternity to eternity.* Some insist His name is *YAHWEH*, but the more well-known title is *JEHOVAH*. In the King James Version of the Bible, Exodus 6:3, Psalms 83:18, Isaiah 12:2, and 26:4 have *JEHOVAH*. Moreover, in the King James Bible Version, *JEHOVAH* sometimes appears as *LORD*—all capitals. When you see *LORD* in any version, it is *JEHOVAH, or YAHWEH*.

One combination is Jehovah-Tsidkeenu—the *LORD OUR RIGHTEOUSNESS*—found in Jeremiah 23:6 and 33:16. That simply means that *JEHOVAH* Himself *IS* our righteousness. And how did that come about? We are told in 2 Corinthians 5:21 that *on the cross Jesus paid the cost* for that blessing, because "God made Jesus, Who [personally] knew no sin, to [actually] become sin for us [in our behalf], so that we might become *THE RIGHTEOUSNESS OF GOD* in Him." *WHO GOD IS DETERMINES WHAT HE DOES. And since God IS always the SAME*, then He will obviously keep *ACTING* the *SAME!*

Jehovah-Mekaddishkem—The *LORD* is our *SANCTIFIER*: Which is found in Exodus 31:13. Now Hebrews 2:11: "Both He Who *SANCTIFIES* and those who are being sanctified are all of One [of God, *in Christ*]." For, in 1 Corinthians 1:30, we read that: "Christ became for us wisdom, righteousness and

SANCTIFICATION." And, that took place on a *TREE!* On the cross, the Savior paid the price to sanctify every person who believes God for that cross-benefit. But, *it was offered to us because of God's sanctifying character that NEVER changes.*

The best-known *JEHOVAH* redemptive title, of course, is the *LORD* our *SHEPHERD*—Jehovah-Rohi—found in Psalms 23:1. Our Savior *claimed to be that Shepherd* in John 10:14: "I [Jesus] am the *GOOD SHEPHERD.*" In 1 Peter 2:25, Jesus was called "The *SHEPHERD* and Overseer of our souls." So, Jesus Christ *LIVED OUT* all of God's redemptive titles.

Yet another redemptive title is Jehovah-Nissi—The *LORD* our *BANNER (VICTOR)*. Exodus 17:15: "Moses built an altar and called its name *THE-LORD-IS-MY-BANNER." LORD* here being *JEHOVAH. And Jesus Christ IS THAT BANNER.* Isaiah 11:10: "The root of Jessie [Jesus] will stand as a *BANNER* to the people." First Corinthians 15:57 also testifies that Jesus Christ is that *BANNER—VICTORY*: "God always gives us the *VICTORY* through our Lord Jesus Christ." That was paid for *BY HIS BLOOD* which He shed upon the cross. In Scripture, the word *BANNER* signifies more than a *FLAG.* It stands for *VICTORY.* True *VICTORY* comes only through Jesus Christ.

Jehovah-Shammah—The *LORD* is there—Or the *LORD* is *PRESENT.* Ezekiel 48:35: "The name of that city [Jerusalem] from that day on will be *THE LORD IS THERE*; or *THE LORD IS PRESENT."* Matthew 28:20 shows how Jesus fulfilled that redemptive title: "*I AM WITH YOU ALWAYS* [all the days]; *to the end of the age."* "Jesus is the same yesterday, today and forever (Hebrews 13:8)." And, God Himself has said: "I *WILL NEVER LEAVE* you nor *FORSAKE* you (Hebrews 13:5-6)."

Jehovah-Sheeloom—The *LORD* is our *PEACE*—Sheeloom means prosperity, health, wholeness, well-being, and peace. Judges 6:24: "Now Gideon built an altar unto the Lord, and called it *THE-LORD-IS-PEACE."* (For spirit, soul and body!)

And once again, Jesus paid the cross-price that provided that blessing *for everyone who will believe for it.* Isaiah 53:5: "The chastisement for [the punishment that purchased] our *PEACE* [Sheeloom—wholeness, health, prosperity well-being and peace] was upon Him [Jesus], and by His bruise we are healed." So Sheeloom has to do with our bodily health. Also see Ephesians 2:14, *which says Jesus Christ is our PEACE.* Romans 15:33: "The God of *PEACE* be with you [believers]." God *ACTS* out of His unchanging redemptive *CHARACTER.*

Another redemptive name of God is Jehovah-Jireh—The *LORD* our *PROVIDER.* Genesis 22:14: "And, Abraham called the name of that place *THE-LORD-WILL-PROVIDE*; just as it is said unto this day: 'In the Mountain of the Lord, it will be provided.'" (Redemptive action based on redemptive nature.)

Again Jesus was connected, because He became poor on the cross, so that we believers might be made *RICH* (that is, *richly supplied with everything we need*—2 Corinthians 8:9). And Philippians 4:19: "*GOD WILL SUPPLY ALL YOUR NEED*, according to His riches in glory *BY JESUS CHRIST.*"

Jehovah-Rapha—The *LORD* our *HEALER*: *God will never back off from His divine-healing-activity, because HE IS THE HEALER. Neither God the Father nor Christ will ever change*, according to Malachi 3:6 and Hebrews 13:8. Exodus 15:26: "I am *THE LORD WHO HEALS.*" And it is "By Christ's bruise [singular] that we are *HEALED* (Isaiah 53:5)." And, Matthew 8:16-17 tells us plainly that Christ took our infirmities, and bore our sicknesses to fulfill Isaiah 53:5. Also, 1 Peter 2:24: "Himself bore our sins in His own body on the tree, that we having died to sins might live for righteousness—by Whose bruise [singular] you were *HEALED.*" So the same price was paid for our bodily healing as for the forgiveness of our sins!

"*ALL* of God's promises in Christ are *YES* (2 Corinthians 1:20)." *Jesus purchased them ALL by His sacrifice!* So Jesus is connected to all of God's *UNCHANGING* redemptive titles.

God cannot alter Who He is—His character or personality. And what He is has been revealed in His plan of redemption and Christ's sacrifice in achieving that redemption upon the cross. Christ's deposit of His blood in heaven is a guarantee that everything He wrought on that cross will ever be intact, and can never be altered, or lose its effectiveness. Thus, the Gospel is the same today as when that blood was deposited.

Chapter Thirteen

Other serious Church of Christ errors—A

This volume is pointing out the fact that *Church of Christ theology is literally riddled with errors—some having serious implications, some being more SILLY than SERIOUS*. Some of those individual errors requiring no entire chapter to cover, then more than one error will appear in this and each of the two following chapters—combining the doctrinal errors that seem best to fit together in each individual chapter.

One inexcusable falsehood of Church of Christ theology is that *the church is the Israel of God*—basing their error on Galatians 6:16, where *Paul did use the term THE ISRAEL OF GOD. But Paul was referring to the TRUE ISRAEL*, which has always been those descendants of Abraham who were *TRUE* to God and to His covenant—not those who were merely the physical offspring of Abraham. In Romans 9:6-8, Paul wrote that: "It is *NOT* that the Word of God has not been effective. For they are not all *TRULY ISRAEL* who are of Israel. *Nor are they children just because they are the offspring of Abraham*: But, in Isaac your seed will be called: Meaning—those who are just children of Abraham's flesh are *NOT* the children of God: For the children of the promise are the [*TRUE*] Seed [of Abraham]." *The Seed of Abraham ultimately refers to Christ*, according to Galatians 3:16. Thus, *the Israel of God is made up of those descendants of Abraham who looked forward to the Messiah*. But, that Church of Christ author insists that Romans 9:6-8 speaks of the *New Testament Church*, not the nation of Israel. That theologian is wrong. Hebrews 8:8 says plainly: "God finding fault with them [those Jews of old], he [Jeremiah, in Jeremiah 31:31-34,] wrote: 'Behold, the days will come,' says the *LORD*, 'that I will make a new covenant with the house of *ISRAEL, AND* with the house of *JUDAH.*'" *Jeremiah's prophecy had to do with ISRAEL and JUDAH; not the New Testament church!* The church has *NEVER* been the Israel of God, and *NEVER* will be. More Bible proof,...

John 1:47 straightens out that Church of Christ author: "Jesus saw Nathanael coming toward Him, and said of him, 'Behold, an *Israelite indeed*, in whom is no deceit!'" "Indeed" means Nathaniel was part of the "Israel of God." For, that is what "Israel of God" means—*a true Israelite—no reference to the New Testament church.* Paul never called the church the "Israel of God." One demonic element of that erroneous idea is that *the church has taken the place of the nation of Israel.* However, God's *ETERNAL PROMISES* to the nation of Israel *fill both Old and New Testaments.* God cannot lie, and many of His promises to Israel have *NOT YET BEEN FULFILLED.*

Such misapplication of "the Israel of God" Bible Truth is *not unique to Church of Christ theology.* That error has been around a long time. But, error is error; so all who hold that error are definitely in error. *Church of Christ flaw upon flaw!*

One more POPULAR error having to do with the church is the unbiblical teaching that the church is the Bride of Christ. Church of Christ theologians fell for that one too. Moreover, numerous other errors have been birthed out of that error. One conclusion is that Israel is the wife of Father God, and the church is the wife of Christ. Under that falsehood, there would be two grooms and two brides—Outright speculation! Nowhere in the Bible is *such nonsense* taught. Besides that, Scripture specifically identifies the Bride of Christ—which is neither the church nor Israel. Instead, that Bride is the New Jerusalem *that will come down from God out of heaven; and so is neither Israel nor the church—both of which are present on the earth NOW. The New Jerusalem will descend from the New Heaven to the New Earth* (Revelation chapter 21). But, *the New Jerusalem will be populated with true believers from Israel, the church, believers who existed before there was an Israel, and everyone who will become a Christian during the Tribulation—after the church has been raptured. NO* believer will be left out. *ALL will be part of the Bride of Christ!*

Another *major falsehood* pushed by the Church of Christ and other religious groups is the teaching that Gentiles are merely *adopted* into Christ. To approximate the Greek word for *adoption,* I offer huiothesia. Pronounce that the best way you can. That word means *SONSHIP*. In the New Testament sense, *SONSHIP* is not about one coming into the world; but instead, *ABOUT ACCEPTING A JEWISH BOY AS AN ADULT*. After the ceremony, the boy could do business just like his father. *He was accepted in the community as an adult.* The word today has a *totally different meaning.* Church of Christ theologians ought to know that from the English dictionary; as well as the Greek dictionary. So, they have no excuse for that error. Scripture is too clear for any doubt about it.

Deceived and deceiving theologians seem to overlook the clear Bible Truth, which Paul plainly pointed out in Romans 9:4—speaking of the "*ISRAELITES, TO WHOM PERTAIN THE ADOPTION*, the glory, the covenants, the giving of the law, the service of God and the promises." So *adoption* pertained to Israel, *not to the church—nor to HOW the Gentiles get into the church.* To get into Christ, both Jews and Gentiles must be born again (John 3:3 and 5-8). Thus, Bible *adoption* has *NOTHING TO DO WITH* how either Jews or Gentiles get into Christ, or the church, but rather with the maturing of those *ALREADY in the church.* Sonship simply means growing up, or maturing, and assuming responsibility as a child of God.

Galatians 4:5: "to redeem those who were *under the law*, that we [Paul including himself] might receive the *adoption as SONS*." Again not talking about how Gentile believers get into the Body of Christ. *Sonship does not make one a family member, but rather positions those already family members.*

Romans 8:15: "You did not receive the spirit of bondage, again unto fear. But, you received the Spirit of *adoption*, by whom we cry out, 'Abba, Father.'" (Both Jews and Gentiles)

Ephesians 1:5: "[God], *having predestined us to adoption as sons by Jesus Christ unto Himself*, according to the good pleasure of His will." (Pertaining to both Jews and Gentiles.)

Romans 8:23: "We who have the first-fruits of the Spirit, even we ourselves, groan within ourselves, eagerly *WAITING* for *the ADOPTION, THE REDEMPTION OF OUR BODY*." Thus *adoption* spoken of here refers to our future resurrection.

Chapter Fourteen

Other serious Church of Christ errors—B

A *MOST* serious error espoused by that Church of Christ author is: *When Adam fell, HIS CONDITION CHANGED, BUT NOT HIS NATURE.* How do highly-educated preachers come up with such unscriptural ideas? His argument contradicts several Scripture passages that teach the very opposite; and we will start consulting those passages right now.

Romans 5:12-14: "Through one man [Adam], sin entered the world [Enough is said right there to *BLAST* that Church of Christ error; but continuing,] and death through sin, and thus, death spread to all men, because all sinned [and they all sinned because Adam's offspring inherited Adam's newly acquired *sinful nature* through his fall. And, get this:]—(For until the law [of Moses was given], sin was in the world, but sin is *NOT* imputed [counted against a person for judgment] where there is no law. Nevertheless, death reigned [in every generation] from Adam to Moses, even over people who had not sinned according to the likeness of the transgression of Adam; *who is a TYPE of Him* [Jesus] Who was to come [into the world]." *Adam's offspring were NOT warned about eating fruit of the forbidden tree: So, they could not violate that law.* Plus, Moses' law (the violation of which would bring death) was not established until many centuries later. So mankind could not break Moses' law. Yet death—the penalty for sin—prevailed in every generation *BETWEEN* those two laws. *The ONLY possible explanation for DEATH prevailing upon earth during all of those centuries is that death was lodged in the human spirit: And that was BECAUSE Adam's offspring had inherited Adam's sin-nature.* Human CONDITION CHANGED because HUMAN NATURE had been altered in Adam's fall!

How could Adam have been a TYPE of Christ? Adam was HEAD of the human race; and Christ is HEAD of the church. Adam was created to reproduce after his kind; and in his fall Adam became a sinner kind—thereafter reproducing sinners.

Romans 5:17-19: "For if by the *ONE* man's [Adam's *ONE*] offense death reigned through that one [Adam], much more, those who receive an abundance of grace, and of the gift of righteousness, will reign in life through *ONE*—Jesus Christ. Therefore, as *through one man's offense judgment came unto all men, resulting in condemnation, even so, through the one Man's righteous act, God's free gift came to all men; resulting in justification of life. By one man's disobedience many were MADE TO BE SINNERS: Also, by one Man's obedience many WILL BE MADE RIGHTEOUS.*" So, Paul explained it in detail. *Adam's NATURE was drastically CHANGED by Adam's fall. Adam's offspring must be just as drastically changed in the opposite direction by the new birth.* Such complete change of nature would not be necessary now, had Adam's nature not become identified with the devil. In Christ, we become *NEW* creatures; shedding our sin-nature (2 Corinthians 5:17-18). Nature-change caused the condition-change.

Romans 3:9: "We have previously proved that both Jews and Greeks are all *UNDER SIN*." Being *UNDER SIN* indicates much more than a mere change of condition. The very term describes a change of nature—in a negative direction.

Ephesians 2:3 tells us plainly that before we were saved, "*We were BY NATURE CHILDREN of wrath.*" Being a *CHILD* involves much more than just experiencing some condition. Romans 6:6 clearly says that we used to be *SLAVES OF SIN. Before Adam sinned, he was not a SLAVE of sin. His slavery came by him CHANGING lords.* Adam bowing to the devil, he became estranged from God—bringing about John 8:44.

John 8:44: "You *ARE OF* your [spiritual] father the devil; and so, the desires of your father you want to do. He was a murderer from the beginning [of his career as God's enemy], and does not stand in the truth [God's Word], because truth does not dwell in him. So, when he tells a lie, he speaks out of his own resources; for he is a liar, and the father of lies."

Through Adam's fall the devil became *the god of this* age (2 Corinthians 4:4): "*The god of this age* [Satan] has blinded the minds of those who do not believe."

Making as little sense as the claim that in the fall *man's nature was not affected, only his condition*, is another claim made by that Church of Christ author—the *PRIESTHOOD* of believers applies *ONLY* to the believer's *status—not function. How can one separate function from status? Status identifies one's position, in which he or she performs certain functions. One example is marriage.* Marriage is definitely a status, but *NOT* without function. *Many functions involved in marriage!* When one lands a job, he or she has a position, or a status; but that position, or status, carries with it responsibility for performing certain functions—*in order to get PAID! And, the term PRIEST automatically brings to mind certain functions. Priests offer sacrifices to God—what New Testament priests are to do.* Status without function would be meaningless!

Another area where that Church of Christ author comes up short is *HIS* contention *that the Bible comes up short on adequately explaining the atonement.* Well, this book points out how that man's 400+ page book comes up very short on explaining a lot of things. *And much of what he does explain contradicts the Bible explanation of the issues he deals with.* Then that man has the *AUDACITY* to claim the Bible shorts us believers on what we need to know about the atonement! *The things I have written in THIS BOOK provide an adequate explanation of the atonement.* And all those things are based upon clear Bible Truth. Put in a Gospel nutshell,...

God created man and gave him a free will. Man used his free will to sin against God, fell from his innocent state, and became identified with Satan. God prophesied that *the Seed of the woman would pay the redemption price to RECONCILE fallen mankind back to God—prophesied throughout the Old Testament and fulfilled in the New.* The entire Bible is full of information about the fall and the atonement. So, where did that theologian get all of his misinformation? And, how dare the man try to push on the rest of us that Church of Christ misinformation? He will have to answer to God for that!

Additional *misinformation* coming from that author is his claim that *Christian ethics are NOT universal—impl*ying *that God does not actually expect sinners to live right.* WHAT???

That author got his information mixed up. The Bible does teach that we Christians are not to attempt to force sinners to live the way we want them to, and punish them if they do not conform to our standards. *Scripture commands believers to leave judgment of sinners up to God!* "Vengeance belongs to God: *He will repay all His enemies!*" (Deuteronomy 32:35, Ezekiel 25:17, Romans 3:5 and 12:19, 2 Thessalonians 1:8, and Hebrews 10:30—and many more similar passages)

That issue came up in the church at Corinth, where *one church member was living IMMORALLY.* Those other church members were tolerating that man committing fornication, and Paul used that incident to teach them that *believers are supposed to deal with immorality going on IN THE CHURCH*; but are to let God deal with those *OUTSIDE THE CHURCH.*

In 1 Corinthians 5:12-13, Paul commented: "What have I [as a Christian] to do with judging those who are *OUTSIDE* [the church]? And, do you believers not judge those who are *INSIDE* [the church, who are sinning]? But, people who are [sinning] outside [the church] *GOD JUDGES*. Therefore, put away from yourselves that evil person." (*Expel him from the church!* And they obviously did cast him out, for later Paul exhorted them to receive him back after he repented. Check out those details in 2 Corinthians 2:6-10.)

Also check out all of these passages that reveal that God does expect all human beings to live according to His Divine standards. Otherwise, how could there be a judgment? That Church of Christ theologian obviously did not even consider these plain passages—*that expose either his ignorance or his dishonesty*—either of which disqualifies him as a teacher.

Isaiah 13:11-12: "I will punish the world for its evil, and the wicked for their iniquity. I will halt the arrogance of the proud, and will lay low the haughtiness of the terrible. I will make a mortal more rare than fine gold." (God the Judge!)

Isaiah 26:21: "The *LORD* comes from His place to punish the inhabitants of the earth for their iniquity: The earth will also disclose her blood, and will no more cover her slain."

Isaiah 66:16: "By fire, and by His sword, the *LORD* will judge *ALL FLESH*: And the slain of the *LORD* will be many." That will be at the end of the present age. In the New Earth, when the inhabitants go home from visiting to worship God, on their way home "they will *LOOK UPON* the corpses of the men who have *TRANSGRESSED* against Me. For their worm does not die, and their fire is not quenched. They will be an abhorrence unto all flesh (Isaiah 66:24)." Christ quoted that very passage in Mark 9:43-49. (Yes, Judgement is coming!)

Jeremiah 25:15-26: "Thus said the *LORD* God of Israel to me: 'Take this wine cup of fury from My hand, and cause *ALL* of the nations to whom I send you to drink it. They will drink, and stagger, and go mad, because of the sword that I will send among them.' So, I took that cup from the *LORD'S* hand, and I made all the nations drink, to whom the *LORD* had sent me—Jerusalem, and the cities of Judah, its kings, and princes, to make them a desolation, an astonishment, and a hissing and a curse, just as it is today: Pharaoh, king of Egypt, his servants, his princes, and all of his people, all the mixed multitude, all the kings of the land of Uz, all the kings of the land of the Philistines (namely, Ashkelon, Gaza, Ekron, and the remnant of Ashdod); and Edom, Moab, and the people of Ammon; all the kings of Tyre; all the kings of Sidon; and the kings of the coastlands which are across the ocean; Dedan, Tema, Buz, and those who are in the farthest corners [of the earth]; the kings of Arabia, and all the kings of the mixed multitude who dwell in the desert; all the kings of Zimri, and all the kings of Elam, and all the kings of the Medes; all of the kings of the north, far and near, one with another; and all the kingdoms of the world which are on the face of the earth. Also, the king of Sheshach will drink after them." (Did God exempt any nation from His judgment?)

Jeremiah 25:28-29: "*It will be that if any of those nations refuse to take that cup from your hand, to drink it*, then you will say unto them, 'Thus says the *LORD* of hosts': "You will certainly drink! For, behold, I begin to bring calamity on the city which is called by My name [Jerusalem], and ought you to be utterly unpunished? *You will not be unpunished*; for I will call for a sword on *ALL* the inhabitants of the earth.""

Jeremiah 25:32-33: "*Behold, DISASTER will go forth from nation unto nation: A great whirlwind will be raised up from the farthest corners of the planet. On that day the slain of the LORD will be from one end of the earth unto the other end of the earth. The dead will not be lamented or gathered or buried; they will become refuse on the ground.*"

Joel 3:2: "I will gather all nations, and bring them down to the Valley of Jehoshaphat: And I will enter into judgment with them there, on account of My own people, My heritage, Israel, whom they have scattered among the nations: They have also divided up My land." (And are still doing it today!)

Joel 3:11-14: "Assemble, and come, all you nations: And gather together all around—*Cause all of Your mighty ones to go down there, LORD*—Let all the nations be awakened and come up to the Valley of Jehoshaphat: For, there I will sit to judge all the surrounding nations. Swing the sickle, for the harvest is now ripe. Come and go down; for the winepress is full. Those wine vats overflow, for their wickedness is great. Multitudes, multitudes in the valley of decision! For the day of the LORD is near in the valley of decision." (*JUDGMENT!*)

Micah 6:8: "*God has shown to you, O MAN, what is good: What does the LORD require of you, but to do justly, to love mercy, and to walk humbly with your God?*" (*EVERYONE!*)

Zephaniah 3:8: "*My determination is to gather ALL of the nations to My assembly of kingdoms—to pour upon them My indignation—all of My fierce anger. And ALL the earth will be devoured with the fire of My jealousy.*" (Now New Testament)

Acts 17:30-31: "The times of ignorance God overlooked, but *NOW commands all men everywhere to repent*—because He has appointed a day on which He will judge the world in righteousness by that Man, Whom He has ordained. He has given assurance of this to all by raising Him from the dead."

Romans 1:18-20: "God's wrath is revealed from heaven *AGAINST ALL UNGODLINESS, and ALL UNRIGHTEOUSNESS* of those people who suppress the truth in unrighteousness;

because what may be known of God is manifest in them, *for God has shown it to them*: Because, since the creation of the world all of His invisible attributes are *CLEARLY* seen; being understood by all the creatures He created; even His eternal power and Godhead, so that they are *ALL* without excuse."

Romans 2:6-11: "He will render to everyone according to his deeds—eternal life to people who by patient continuance in doing good, seek for glory, honor, and immortality; but to all of those who are self-seeking, and do not obey the truth, but, obey unrighteousness—indignation, wrath, tribulation, and anguish on *EVERY* soul of those who do evil, of the Jew first, and also of the Greek. But, glory, honor, and peace to everyone who works what is good; to the Jew first, and also to the Greek. For there is *NO PARTIALITY* with God."

Second Thessalonians 1:6-9: "It is a righteous thing with God to repay with tribulation those who trouble you, and to give you who are troubled rest with us when the Lord Jesus comes back from heaven with His mighty angels; *in flaming fire taking vengeance upon those who do not know God, and those who do not obey the Gospel of our Lord Jesus Christ.* They will be punished with everlasting destruction from the presence of the Lord and from the glory of His power."

Jude 14-15: "Enoch, the seventh from Adam, prophesied about these men also, saying: 'Behold, the Lord comes with ten thousands of His saints, to execute judgment on *ALL*; to convict all who are ungodly among them of all their ungodly deeds, which they have committed in an ungodly way, and convict them of all the harsh things, which ungodly sinners have spoken against Him.'" (*Sin is wrong for everybody!*)

Does God's Word say murder, theft, adultery, lying, etc. are okay for sinners, but not okay for Christians? *Christian ethics are for every human being; not just for saved people!*

I have observed that the religious institutions that claim they are the *ONLY God-approved church* are the very groups that hold the *weirdest and most unscriptural doctrines*. And the Church of Christ is one of those groups—one which has *the most unscriptural theology*—but a group which is highly respected in much of the church world. *And many believers will likely scold me for writing the things I have written about the Church of Christ within this book*—exposing their MANY doctrinal errors, and their OUTRIGHT DISHONESTY.

The Church of Christ is not the only deceived group. The *Calvinist* theology is an even worse deception. I have written three books exposing Calvinism—*in which I have uncovered the outright lies of that demonic theology*—proving Calvinism is *A CONSPIRACY* and *A DELUSION*. And, one book proving that *Christians are NOT saved sinners*. You can see them all by clicking on www.livingwayfellowshiponline.org.

However, what the "Shepherd's Chapel" ministry teaches is the most diabolical doctrine of all. My latest book exposes the gross heresies of Shepherd's Chapel. *It is hard to believe that so many people have been BLINDED by their weird and unbiblical doctrines.* That book also exposes the *gross errors of some other religious groups*. It uncovers lots of the devil's hiding-places. (Religion, politics, entertainment, etc., etc.)

I know there are still others out there who teach ungodly things, but I cannot write about them all—and do not know about all of them that are out there. Nothing *NEW*, however; for about 1900 years ago John said in 1 John 4:1: "Beloved, believe not every spirit, but rather, test the spirits, whether they are of God; because many false prophets have gone out into the world." If that was happening in John's day, then it happens today too! *And that problem was not prevalent only in heathen religions, but in Christian churches as well. Over many centuries deceived preachers have done much damage within the church.* And the devil's shenanigans will continue right up to the very end—prophesied throughout Scripture. Be not deceived by religious falsehoods, but be alert, just as the apostle John admonished 1900 years ago.

That 400+ page Church of Christ doctrine manual spews out more gross errors than those I pointed out already. And some of those more serious errors are dealt with in the next chapter—along with the biblical proof that they are errors.

Chapter Fifteen

Other serious Church of Christ errors—C

Another serious error espoused by that Church of Christ author is the *lumping together* of all kinds of sufferings. *The man suggests that Christians are not exempt from any of the sufferings which are COMMON to the human race*—obviously referring to sickness, poverty, and the like. And, the Church of Christ is not the only religious group holding that sort of teaching. *THEY ARE ALL IN ERROR*—Because, on the cross, Jesus Christ suffered all of those kinds of human sufferings on our behalf; *for the purpose of delivering us believers from all of those types of sufferings. THE ONLY* suffering our Lord did not deliver us from is persecution. Thus, when Paul and Peter in their letters mention Christian suffering, both refer to *persecution for the faith—NOT* to sickness, poverty or any other of those many curses which our Savior suffered in our place; *so that we believers do not have to suffer those things.* Deuteronomy chapter twenty-eight lists all the curses Jesus Christ *BECAME* while on that cross—according to Galatians 3:13. *Paul taught that Jesus actually BECAME A CURSE ON THE CROSS*, and thereby removed the curses from all those who *BELIEVE* God's Word, instead of trying to explain away the *MIRACULOUS* portions of the Gospel with their *gutless, demon-inspired theology.* Many Christians suffer needlessly; and *I have written a book addressing that problem. The book differentiates between genuine Christian suffering and what is not. If a Christian suffering sickness is suffering FOR THE LORD, then the same would be true for a sinner. But, that is not so.* Again, see www.livingwayfellowshiponline.org to find out more about that enlightening book, and several others.

Sickness is not counted Christian suffering in the eyes of God. It is a shame that many theologians had rather put up with sickness in their own bodies; and in the bodies of their church members—sickness which Jesus Christ endured on the cross, in order to deliver Christians from—than to suffer persecution for the faith, *which the Savior did not redeem us from*. While that author does teach that believers will suffer persecution for the faith, he essentially puts sickness in the same category—suffering for God. But having the flu or any other sickness does not glorify Christ. Divine healing does!

I do need to point out that believers are not exempt from sickness *just because they are Christians*. But, believers *DO HAVE* New Covenant benefits available to them that sinners *DO NOT HAVE; unless those sinners become New Testament believers too*. By Christ's wound on that tree we were healed (Isaiah 53:4-5, Matthew 8:17, Galatians 3:13, 1 Peter 2:24).

The man's commentary on Paul's words in 1 Corinthians 5:5—turn that sinning church member over to Satan for the *destruction of the flesh*—is that the "destruction of the flesh" actually meant the elimination of the man's sinful attitudes and tendencies. Now, I cannot speak for you, but I have not found anywhere in the Bible that the devil has the tendency to eliminate sinful attitudes and tendencies. *The devil is the one that incites evil attitudes and tendencies! Paul obviously meant infliction of sickness on the man's physical body.* The idea was to put him under Satan's full power of destruction, *so that the man just might come to his senses, REPENT, and be restored to fellowship with both God and the church.*

One more major flaw of that author is his insistence that despite what Jesus Christ plainly said in Matthew 12:31-32 and Mark 3:28-29, *about blasphemy against the Holy Spirit being an unforgivable sin*, there is *NO UNFORGIVABLE SIN*. He contends that what the Lord meant was that the one who blasphemes against the Holy Spirit will become callused, will not repent, and for that reason alone will remain unforgiven. However, in Matthew and Mark, the Savior said that *EVERY* blasphemy will be forgiven—*EXCEPT* blasphemy against the Holy Spirit. Surely, Christ did not mean that all other kinds of blasphemy will *AUTOMATICALLY BE FORGIVEN*: One has to repent in order to be forgiven for any blasphemy. That is a given. Christ did *NOT* differentiate between *SINS REPENTED OF AND SINS NOT REPENTED OF*. His obvious concern was with *WHO* the blasphemy was against. Think about that!

Still another error is that man's insistence that the *little ones* whom Jesus said "believe on Me" *were NOT actual little children, BUT instead ADULT believers*. But if they had been believing adults, why did the Lord call them *little ones? That makes NO SENSE—scriptural or otherwise.* Matthew 18:1-6: "The disciples came to Jesus, saying, 'Who is greatest in the kingdom of heaven?' Then, Jesus called a *little child* to Him, set him in the midst of the disciples, and then said to them, 'Unless you are converted and become as little children, you *WILL BY NO MEANS* enter the kingdom of heaven. Whoever humbles himself as *this little child* is the greatest one in the kingdom of heaven. Moreover, whoever receives a *little child like this one* [He had set in their midst] in My name receives Me. But, whoever causes one of these *little ones who believe in Me* to commit sin, it would be better for him if a millstone were hung around his neck, and he were to be drowned in the depth of the sea.'" The *little ones* Christ kept mentioning were obviously *little children* who believed on Him; not adult believers. *Preachers just believe what they WANT to believe!*

One of the most unscriptural and arrogant claims of the Church of Christ is that prospective church members must be examined and trained by church authorities before being *GRANTED* church membership. That may sound like sound doctrine, *but how biblical is it?* If you will remember, on the Day of Pentecost, three thousand *NEW* believers were added unto the new-born church. There was no time for Church of Christ *examination and instruction.* See Acts 2:41. And Acts 2:47: *"The Lord added unto the church daily those who were being saved."* The Lord, not the church, did the adding. And Matthew 28:19-20 says Christ commanded His followers to *make disciples FIRST; THEN teach them.* Teach them what? *To continue THE SAME ministry He performed on earth until His return!* Thus, a *MIRACLE MINISTRY* (Matthew 10:1, 7-8).

A related *CLAIM* by that book author is that, the original apostles were called and ordained by the Lord Jesus Christ. But, thereafter, *the church chose and placed church leaders.* The church did chose Phillip to be a deacon, but God chose him to be an evangelist. *It is the Holy Spirit Who distributes ministry gifts; not the church!* See 1 Corinthians 12:11. The church is involved, but it must seek Holy Spirit guidance in all that it does. *Not many churches do that today—especially the Church of Christ. Without Holy Spirit guidance, how may church leaders know WHO HAS WHAT Holy-Spirit-ministry?* They cannot prove it one way or the other, so you just have to take their word for it. *How religiously convenient!*

In his book, the author does propose that the Holy Spirit qualifies and calls people into ministry today. But elsewhere *the man denies the MIRACULOUS MANIFESTATIONS of Holy Spirit ministry.* So how would anyone truly know if a church leader is called and empowered by the Holy Spirit? In early days of the church one's Holy Spirit calling was self-evident. Paul talked about people who have a *FORM* of godliness but *DENY* the power thereof—telling us to turn away from such people (2 Timothy 3:5). *And his word is good to this day!*

Over and over in his book, that Church of Christ author portrayed the church as community, whereas, in Scripture, the church is pictured as a body—the Body of Christ on the earth. *The word community appears many times in his book, but, I found community NOT ONCE in Strong's concordance.* Community is made up of many residents—*who may move away at any time.* But the human body, as well as the Body of Christ, is made up of many members; *which we hope will never vacate either our physical body, or the Body of Christ. Community members may be connected by various interests, but their life does not depend upon their staying in the same community.* On the other hand, *Body-of-Christ-members* are joined together by *LIFE*; just as our *physical-body-members* are. While community residents may sometimes be helpful, our physical-body-members are essential. And so are all the members of the Body of Christ. Paul had much to say about our physical bodies and the Body of Christ in 1 Corinthians chapter twelve. You will surely want to read and absorb it.

Now, let us look at some *REALLY SILLY* Church of Christ doctrines. *HOW* do preachers come up with such ridiculous concepts? I get embarrassed *FOR THEM* upon reading some of their ridiculous comments on certain subjects—like some of the following. They would be humorous, if not so tragic.

Chapter Sixteen

Some silly Church of Christ doctrines

Whereas certain Church of Christ doctrines have serious implications, others are more silly than serious. *And certain ones are actually a combination of silly and serious*—like the claim that Genesis 3:15 is God's answer to why people hate snakes—*RATHER THAN BEING A PROPHECY* of the Savior's sacrifice on the cross. Genesis 3:14-15: "And the LORD God said to *THE SERPENT* [an actual snake]: 'Because you have done this [being used by the devil to cause man to fall], you are cursed more than all cattle; more than any other animal of the field: *On your belly you will go* [from now on]: And you will eat *DUST* all the days of your life. Also, I will put enmity between you and the woman, and between your seed [your offspring] and her Seed—*He will bruise your head, and you will bruise His heel.*'" Although I have heard other preachers make the same claim, that Church of Christ author teaches the same falsehood. God did not say that snakes will bruise the heel of every human being: Just *HIS* heel. Moreover, not every human being will bruise the heads of snakes: Just *HE will bruise the Serpent's head.* And more than that, God was obviously addressing the devil in that statement, because in Revelation 20:2, the devil is referred to as *the Serpent of old.* Anyway, why would God make such a fuss over the conflict between snakes and people. *He would NOT WASTE His time commenting on the man-snake problem.* No, our Creator was addressing a *SERIOUS* issue—*prophesying the coming of the Messiah, and His mission on the earth.* Thus, *in his religious SILLINESS, that author made a SERIOUS mistake in the way he handled that passage.* (Both silly and serious)

In addition, God made that observation right after Adam and Eve had sinned in the Garden of Eden. But, evidently, animal hostility did not arise until *AFTER* the flood of Noah. Genesis 9:2-3: "[From now on] the fear of you and the dread of you will be on every animal of the earth, on every bird of the air, on all that moves on the earth, and on all the fish of the seas. They are given into your hand. Every moving thing that lives on earth will be food for you. I have given you *ALL* things [*including meat*], even as I gave you the green herbs." That had to be the time animals began to both fear and eat one another, just as they began to fear and attack humans.

On the New Earth God will *RESTORE* the *non-aggressive nature of all animals as it was in the beginning*: Isaiah 11:7: "The cow and the bear will graze together. Their young ones will lie down together; *the lion will eat straw just like the ox.*" Isaiah 65:25: "The wolf and the lamb will feed together. The lion will eat straw like the ox. *But DUST will be the serpent's food*. They will not hurt or destroy in all My holy mountain."

And the devil does have *spiritual offspring*: In John 8:44, Jesus said that *those people were of their FATHER the devil*. Now every human being has a natural father—a man. Thus, the only way Satan can be someone's father is in a spiritual sense. John said plainly in 1 John 3:1: "In this the *children* of the devil and the *children* of God are manifest." Thus, the devil (also known as Satan) has spiritual children—the seed of the Serpent. *So God was not referring to snake-hate!*

Christ was also identified as the Seed in Galatians 3:16: "Now to Abraham and his Seed were the promises made. He does not say, 'And to seeds,' as of many, but as of one: 'And to your Seed,' Who is Christ." Christ was called the Seed of Abraham; and must also be the woman's Seed spoken of in Genesis 3:15—*making that a prophesy of the cross event.*

Now a super-silly claim by that Church of Christ author: John 2:14-15: "And the Lord found in the temple those who sold oxen, and sheep, and doves, and those moneychangers doing business. When Christ had made a whip of cords, He *DROVE* them all out of the temple, along with the sheep and oxen, and poured out the changers' money, and overturned their tables." That author said that *Jesus whipped not those moneychangers, but the animals! He would not be so cruel to human beings.* But I have to ask: "*Were those animals guilty of wrong-doing?*" The moneychangers were the GUILTY ones! *Why would Jesus Christ whip those innocent animals for the sins committed by those guilty human beings*? Other Gospel writers recorded the *SAME EVENT*, and made it more clear. Matthew 21:12: "Jesus went into the temple, and *drove out all those who bought and sold in the temple*, and overturned the tables of the moneychangers and the seats of those who sold doves." Why did that author not use *THAT* passage? Or Mark 11:15: "Then Jesus went into the temple and *began to drive out THOSE who bought and sold in the temple* [people, not the innocent animals they were buying and selling], and He also overturned the tables of those moneychangers, and the seats of *those who sold* doves." Luke 19:45: "Then Jesus went into the temple, and began to drive out all *those who bought and sold* in the temple." *NOTHING* was said in any of these passages about Jesus whipping those animals. (*Silly!*)

Tithing: I found no reference to tithing by that Church of Christ author, but in another book pushing the doctrines of that church I found lots of lies about tithing. The basic lie is that tithing was tied to the Old Testament. So when the Old Testament was *DONE AWAY WITH, TITHING WENT WITH IT.* That is an outright lie—and I will tell you why!

First of all, tithing was practiced by God's faithful people *LONG BEFORE* Moses' law was instituted: Which means the Church of Christ preachers are either ignorant, or big liars.

Genesis 14:18-20: "Melchizedek, King of Salem, brought out bread and wine [to Abram and all of those with him]: *He was the priest of God Most High.* And he blessed Abram and said: 'Blessed be Abram, of God Most High, the Possessor of heaven and earth: And blessed be God Most High, Who has delivered all your enemies into your hand.' And *Abram gave him* [Melchizedek] *a tithe of all.*" *LONG BEFORE Moses' law!*

Genesis 28:20-22: "Then, Jacob made a vow: 'If God will be with me and keep me in the way I am going, and give me bread to eat, and clothing to put on, so that I come back to my father's house in peace, then the *LORD* will be my God. And this stone I have set up as a pillar will be God's house; and *of all that You give me, I will surely give a tenth to You.*'" *The law only structured the already-existing tithing practice.*

Tithing actually began earlier. Genesis 4:2-5: "Abel was a *keeper of sheep*, while Cain was a *tiller of the ground. And in the process of time, Cain brought an offering to the LORD OF THE FRUIT OF the ground. Abel brought OF THE FIRSTBORN OF HIS FLOCK and its fat.* The LORD respected Abel and his offering, but He did not respect Cain and his offering."

Why did God respect Abel's offering, but not Cain's? *The offering of Abel was the firstborn or FIRST-FRUIT of his flock.* That is what the *TITHE* is—the first-fruit of all our increase. *Cain brought OF the fruit of the ground.* It was not said that Cain brought the *FIRST-FRUIT* of his crops. Proverbs 3:9-10 says: "*HONOR* the *LORD* with all your possessions; with the *first-fruit of your increase*; and then your barns will be filled with plenty, and your vats will overflow with new wine." The problem was not Cain offering vegetables, rather than meat. *Tithing HONORS the Creator. Was HONORING God supposed to cease with the replacement of the Old Testament?*

NOT ONLY does failing to tithe *DISHONOR GOD, IT ALSO ROBS* Him. Look at Malachi 3:8-9: "*Will a man rob God?* Yet you have robbed Me [God]! But, you ask, 'In what way have we robbed You?' In *TITHES* and offerings. So you are cursed with a curse, because you have *ROBBED* Me." If not tithing *ROBBED* God back then, does it not still *ROB* God today?

Abraham gave tithes to Melchizedek—the priest of God in Abraham's day. Hebrews 5:10: "[Jesus Christ was] called by God *A HIGH PRIEST AFTER THE ORDER OF MELCHIZEDEK, WHO RECEIVED TITHES.*" "*After the ORDER of Melchizedek*" has to mean that as God's High Priest Jesus receives tithes. Otherwise, how could Jesus Christ be called "*after the order of Melchizedek*"? (That error too is both silly and serious.)

One more silly: That Church of Christ book-author, just like many other preachers, used the common phrase: "*Back in New Testament times.*" Are we not still in New Testament times? If not, then what dispensation are we in? We are not in the Millennium or the New Earth! We are definitely not in the Old Testament. So, we have to be in the New Testament. Theologians are not as smart as they want us to believe.

Chapter Seventeen

Miscellaneous misunderstandings

Packing several other Church of Christ religious flaws in this chapter, the first will be *the RULE that church members MUST partake of the Lord's Supper EVERY Sunday.* Not only that, *it has to be done in one of THEIR church meetings.* And, *only Church of Christ members are allowed to participate in their communion*; for they believe that non-Church-of-Christ church members are not part of the real church—the Body of Christ. But what does the *BIBLE* say about all of that. *NO Scripture passage DEMANDS that Christians partake of the Lord's Supper EVERY week.* Christ's actual words were: "*As OFTEN as you do this, do it in REMEMBRANCE of Me.*" Paul made that clear in 1 Corinthians 11:23-25. *MORE important than the FREQUENCY of participating in the Lord's Supper is remembering to do it "IN REMEMBRANCE OF HIM."* And that means laying hold of the benefits our Savior wrought for us in His sacrifice on the tree. Hebrews 2:14 tells us about one of the *MAJOR* benefits of Christ's crucifixion—rendering the devil ineffective to *believing Christians.* The Lord's Supper is not to be taken just out of religious duty. Paul told believers in Corinth that, *being ignorant of the purpose of communion, but partaking of it anyway, was the CAUSE of many of them being SICK, and dying early* (1 Corinthians 11:27-30). So, if taking communion *in an unworthy manner* was the cause of sickness among them back then—or among us today—*then our partaking of communion with the proper attitude ought to bring healing!* I know Church of Christ congregations which have many sick members. So, what does that tell you about their *REAL* understanding of the Lord's Supper? If Paul was correct about bringing judgment on oneself by partaking of the Lord's Supper in *an unworthy manner, then many today obviously have little understanding of the Lord's Supper. The Gospel is not to be engaged in out of mere religious duty.* We read in John 4:23-24 that God is looking for people who will worship Him in spirit and truth—not just in outward acts.

85

Still another un-called for rule in the Church of Christ is that the use of musical instruments in church meetings is a big no-no. *They claim that there are no references in the New Testament to musical instruments being USED in any church meeting.* While that may be so, *the word PSALMS does occur in the New Testament* (Ephesians 5:19, Colossians 3:16 and James 5:13). And if you will check word numbers 5567 and 5568 in Strong's New Testament Dictionary, in the back of Strong's Concordance, you will discover that *the very WORD psalms means words set to music.* So, musical instruments were definitely meant to be involved in singing psalms; and that in church meetings, where psalms are usually sung.

One of their arguments is that singing psalms is *making melody in your heart* (Ephesians 5:19). *That would eliminate musical instruments.* But, *it would also eliminate your voice.* Musical instruments were prominent in the temple-worship in the past under King David and following kings: And there will be harps in heaven (Revelation 5:8, 14:2 and 15:2). *But God does not approve of music in church meetings now???*

One of the problems with that stance is that *those same people teach it is okay to play musical instruments OUTSIDE church meetings.* Some of them *EVEN* have their own music band. But, *the meeting-house is not the church anyway.* The real Church is the *PEOPLE* who meet in the meeting-house. Why would music be wrong *IN* church, but right elsewhere? *The Church of Christ FOCUSES on the building, not believers.* God is interested in believers, *NOT MEETING-HOUSES!*

My wife and I attended one of their meetings. *The song leader announced the first song and then took out his PITCH PIPE, to make sure they all got on the right key.* When I saw him do that, I yelled out on the inside of me: *That pitch pipe is a musical instrument! It might be small, and only one, but that is still a musical instrument used in church!* But,...

This is not about musical instruments, and buildings, but about being honest instead of being hypocritical. The Church of Christ preachers claim that: *Where the Bible speaks they speak; where the Bible is silent they are silent.* Believers met either in the temple, or in people's residences, in those early years. *There is nothing in the New Testament about buildings being set aside for church meetings! That began in the fourth century under Constantine.* However, every Church of Christ congregation either owns or is paying for *a BUILDING THEY HAVE SET ASIDE for the specific purpose of church meetings.* Thus, they do speak where the Bible is silent. *HYPOCRITES!*

One more *misunderstanding* I must deal with is common among many denominations today—*That women cannot be in Gospel ministry; and that it is even a SHAME for women to speak in church meetings. I am aware that those very words are recorded in most Bible translations; but a question arises about whether Paul himself was making a NEW rule, or was quoting the words of some Jewish rabbi who had a low view of women—and Paul refuting his words.* Most versions begin verse 34 of 1 Corinthians 14 with "*As in all the churches, let your women keep silent, for they are not permitted to speak.*" But a different Bible version tacks "as in all the churches of the saints" onto verse thirty-three, *AND THEN BEGINS* verse thirty-four: "*Let your women keep silent in the churches, for they are not permitted to speak.*" That word shift shows that *Paul separated the words in verses thirty-four and thirty-five from the ones he wrote earlier.* Moreover, Paul blurted out in verse thirty-six: "Did the Word of God come from you?"—As though what he had just written was actually a quote of the believers in Corinth, who had quoted someone else. In other words, *Paul seems to start questioning the very genuineness of the words in verses thirty-four and thirty-five.* For back in chapter eleven, Paul talked about *women prophesying*. Well, *prophesying would make sense only in some public meeting. Did women prophesy in the open streets, but not in church? And, if Paul's words are taken LITERALLY, as soon as those women enter the meeting-house, they need to ZIP THEIR LIP, and utter no sound until they exit the meeting-house.* Women *DO* talk in church, so they *DO NOT* heed all of Paul's words.

This book is not designed for an in-depth explanation of the subject of Christian women's God-approved functions in the church. However, I will recommend a book that does go into detail about that—"*WHO SAID WOMEN CAN'T TEACH?*"

The author is *Charles Trombley*; Bridge Logos the publisher. That author goes into detail about what I introduced above, and includes much more than I can deal with in this book. The subject was brought up only because it is a sore spot in many denominations—including the Church of Christ. And, the Church of Christ is a denomination whether or not they admit it. *Maybe not in a legal sense; but their CONTROL over those SUPPOSEDLY INDEPENDENT CHURCHES proves they are definitely a denomination in that CONTROL sense.*

In Christ, there is neither male nor female. In the home, the husband is head of the wife, and bears responsibility for the family. In the writings of the "Early Church Fathers" the record reveals that *at least during the first four centuries the Gospel ministry was not restricted to men: Women exercised the same spiritual gifts as men—IN the church and BEYOND.*

A final issue in this chapter: From cover to cover in that Church of Christ doctrinal dissertation, I noticed the author emphasized the human *mind, will* and *emotions*; with much less emphasis upon the *SPIRIT*. Even when discussing faith, the man failed to connect one's faith with one's spirit. Bible faith is of the spirit—*the very core of humanity*. Even though Jesus taught that we must love God with our *WHOLE* spirit, soul, mind and strength (Mark 12:30), *our spirit is at the top of the list!* God works from the inside to the outside.

Spirit being the very core of human beings, the core was where our human problem lay; and therefore what our Lord primarily dealt with on the cross. *Every other problem stems from that core-problem. Since all other human problems come from the core-problem within our spirit, the SOLUTION has to be applied WITHIN our spirit.* The solution is the *RE-BIRTH* of our human spirit. And, *the rebirth of the human spirit can ONLY be accomplished by spiritual power—the Holy Spirit of God.* Water not being a spiritual power, water cannot cause the new birth of one's spirit. *Baptism in water is an outward action which touches only the body. So there is no connection between one's physical BODY being immersed in water and one's SPIRIT being re-birthed.* That is just a taste of the final wrap up, so be sure to soak it all in.

Conclusion

Summary of the principle parts

This will *NOT* be a mere rehash of the foregoing material. And, even before we proceed to the *CORE* of this *condensed conclusion,* let me point out another *vital truth* that will help explain the reasons for going over this concluding material; *plus vital information not previously included.*

Remember that I said earlier that the author of that 400+ *page Church of Christ doctrine book wrote some good things; but I said little of what those good things were the man said.* The author of that book deserves credit for *rejecting the core principles of Calvinism. The Church of Christ is definitely not Calvinist; at least regarding Calvin's core theology known as TULIP.* I have written three books that *EXPOSE* that heresy. On our website www.livingwayfellowshiponline.org, you can view those books on *CALVINISM;* as well as the books I have written on Bible Realities about other vital issues—a total of nine books. This will be the tenth. And, I know the modern church needs them *ALL,* because they *ALL* touch on *touchy topics* much of the modern church is either grossly ignorant about, or actually rail against—Essential Bible Truths, vital to our well-being. It will not hurt to check them out.

The Church of Christ, *just as many other denominations,* does hold to *PART* of Calvin's heretical doctrines—*especially the part about miracle-ministry being suspended AFTER the first century.* And *BOTH* Calvinists and the Church of Christ endeavor to support *THEIR* theological stance by *pushing to the max one Scripture passage*—1 Corinthians 13:8-10. But verses 11-12 expose and destroy the utter *FALLACY* of their biased interpretation of verses 8-10. And they have no other scriptural evidence that supposedly supports their theology. They always turn to that one passage, and make comments about it that are simply not true. They read their lies into it, and expect us to take their *educated* (???) word for it.

Numerous other passages prove beyond doubt that their *BIASED conclusions* about 1 Corinthians 13:8-10 *are merely that—BIASED.* For, *there is ABSOLUTELY NO BIBLE TRUTH in their distorted claims.* Their contention is that, when Paul said, "When that which is perfect has come," he was talking about *the completion of the New Testament writings.* Psalms 19:7 says that the law of the Lord *IS PERFECT—referring to the Old Testament books.* Moreover, James 1:25 talks about *the PERFECT LAW of liberty, referring to the New Testament books which existed in James' day.* The last New Testament books came much later. So there is no way Paul was talking about the *COMPLETION of the New Testament* by his words, "When that which is perfect has come, that which is in part will be done away." *Now, that which is in part DOES REFER to the Holy-Spirit-gifts of tongues, and prophecy.* They surely will *CEASE* when the perfect has arrived. But, *the PERFECT Paul prophesied about was the NEXT AGE*—not the last New Testament book. For Paul plainly wrote that when that time would come, he would "know, even as he was known." *Paul died long before the New Testament was complete. So, Paul either knew not what he was talking about, told a big lie, or was referring to something other than book-writing.*

In John 14:12, Jesus promised that those who believe on Him will do the same works He did in His ministry on earth. He did not limit that promise to the first century Christians, nor to the twelve apostles: *"WHOEVER believes on Him!"*

In Matthew 28:18-20, Jesus commanded His disciples to make more disciples, *and then TEACH them to do everything He had commanded those first disciples to do in ministry.* He then promised that He would be with them to the end of the age. *That FIRST generation did not live to the END of the age. So that was Christ's promise to believers right up to the END of the present age.* And, Matthew chapter 10 lists the things *Jesus commanded those first disciples to perform in ministry.* That list includes: *Healing the sick, cleansing lepers, raising the dead,* and *casting out demons. That is what Jesus Christ commanded that first generation of believers to perform; and that same command holds to this day; and will hold until our Lord returns. So, the Spiritual gifts and ministries WILL NOT CEASE before then; but are available to all who believe now!*

Moreover, 1 Corinthians 12:28 tells us that *God has SET* in the church apostles, prophets, teachers, miracles, gifts of healing, etc., etc. That Greek word translated *SET* means to *APPOINT, ESTABLISH, ORDAIN*. And that means those gifts and ministries were *permanently SET in the church*; and are to remain until this age is over. In the next age miracles will not be needed. But, they are greatly needed in this age. Also notice that *Paul used the very same word, "SET," to describe ALL of the gifts and ministries*. Thus, *if ONE of those gifts or ministries was meant to be permanent, then ALL were meant to be permanent*. In Ephesians 4:11-13, Paul again said that the Lord gave to the church *apostles, prophets, evangelists, pastors*, and *teachers*. Once again, *if ONE of those ministries was meant to be permanent, then ALL of them were meant to be permanent. Carry out all of your arguments to their logical scriptural conclusions*. For, *no prophecy of Scripture is of any PRIVATE interpretation* (2 Peter 1:20-21). Also, Hebrews 2:4 says that *GOD BORE WITNESS TO THE GOSPEL MESSAGE in early days with signs, wonders, miracles, and Holy Spirit gifts, according to His will, which changes not* (Malachi 3:6). *Why would He not confirm His Word in the same way today?*

The primary purpose of this book is to expose the primary doctrines of the Church of Christ as heresy; and to show that plainly from multiple Scripture passages. In this conclusion I will tackle only the highlights of their primary doctrine, and then add a few comments not made earlier. In John chapter three, the Lord mentioned nothing about water-baptism. *He only addressed the concerns of Nicodemus about his natural birth.* Right up front Jesus said one must be born *AGAIN* in order to enter God's Kingdom. The word *AGAIN* must mean an additional birth. *And, not another birth of the same kind, but a birth of a higher order—Because the Greek word Jesus used there actually means FROM ABOVE.* He used the same word in John 19:11, when He told Pilate that he could have no authority over Him unless it was given *from above*. Thus, Christ contrasted two different kinds of birth—natural and spiritual. He settled that in John 3:6 when He said: *What is born of flesh is flesh, and what is born of Spirit is spirit. Had the Lord been teaching the necessity of water-baptism in the new birth, verse six would not have made any sense.*

Moreover, the Church of Christ theologians contend that Titus 3:5 teaches that water-baptism is part of the salvation process: For "Jesus saved us by the *washing of regeneration and renewing of the Holy Spirit.*" But, there is no mention of baptism in that Scripture! Nor, even any reference to water! The word for washing is totally different. However, the main point is that: Both the words, and sentence construction, in that passage *PROVE* that it is *regeneration that produces the washing—not washing that produces regeneration.* Consider the next part of that verse—"*the renewing of the Holy Spirit.*" Does the renewing produce the Holy Spirit; or does the Holy Spirit produce the renewing? *The answer should be obvious.* And it is the same for Paul's earlier statement. Regeneration produces the washing: *Regeneration IS the washing!* Look at Revelation 1:5: "Jesus washed us from our sins by His own blood." Same family of Greek words. *Only the blood of Jesus can take away sins.* Water cannot touch the inner man.

The final wrap up: How can the church be profited when its preachers teach a few good things, *but their foundational doctrines actually oppose the Holy Scriptures*—and therefore must be detrimental to the church? They have to have some bait, so to speak, in order to persuade the church members that they are in the *right church—so that they will be loyal to BOTH the denomination, and its theology.* That book author contends that *there is only one Christ and therefore only one church*—the Church of Christ. Both this book, and the Bible itself, prove otherwise—conclusively. This is not about some difference of opinion between preachers, or denominations. This is about Bible Truth versus church leader error. Thus, the stakes are much too high for preachers to tamper with. *People's ETERNAL well-being is in the balance.* That is what the devil is after—using religion to achieve his evil agenda.

I recommend another book of mine, which exposes many UNIQUE places the devil has found to HIDE in—detrimental doctrines PUSHED by some other deceived preachers. Think not that such deception is not running rampant in the church TODAY. Paul, Peter, and others warned about deception in the last days. Let us be smart enough to heed the warnings. To see that book, go to www.livingwayfellowshiponline.org.

www.ingramcontent.com/pod-product-compliance
Lightning Source LLC
LaVergne TN
LVHW011849060526
838200LV00054B/4247